Black-Eyed

PEAS

TO

PRALINES

TEXAS STYLE

Barbara C. Jones
1901 South Shore Drive
Bonham, Texas 75418
903/583-8898

Cover Photograph by
Richard Reynolds

First Printing   1991   5,000
Second Printing   1991   5,000

ISBN 0-9630404-0-5

Printed in the USA by
WIMMER BROTHERS
A Wimmer Company
Memphis • Dallas

Introduction

We Texans are a hardy bunch and we sure like to eat! Now, just in case someone thought we only ate barbecue and chili, this cookbook will serve as a guide to a large variety of Texas foods. Of course, barbecue and chili are not only a "stick-to-the ribs" food, they are foods that serve a purpose. Barbecues and chili-cooking can be "happenings". They serve as the basis for parties, backyard cooking, cook-offs, festivals, rodeos, competitions and many other get-togethers. This one Texas book cannot do barbecue or chili justice since there must be as many recipes for them as there are bluebonnets in the Texas Hill Country in spring.

Another food that is a Texas classic is, of course, chicken-fried steak! In Texas our babies' first solid food is a hamburger and fries and the love for hamburgers goes on through life. But, by the age of 6, those kids expand their tastes to include chicken-fried steak and from that age on, chicken-fried steak is a staple. And don't forget, anytime the cook serves chicken-fried steak without the cream gravy, he is in deep trouble. Would you believe that approximately 90% of the 4000 members of the Texas Restaurant Association in Texas offer this Texas delicacy on their menu? Let's show them up and cook it ourselves.

Naturally, you've noticed the name of this cookbook. The variety of Texas foods goes from black-eyed peas, whether in the form of a dip, hot with jalapenos or a salad to the sweet Mexican praline, whether it be a candy, a praline cake or a sweet caramelly praline bar. We like almost everything from the lowly pinto bean to the scrumptious fresh, strawberry cheesecake (better than New York ever thought about making). We like the simple Calico salad and the crunch of the water chestnut added to the broccoli casserole. We take pride in the authority of the jalapeno and the comfort of the old-fashioned apple pie. Don't forget the "fresh from the garden" fried okra or the "fresh from the pool" fried catfish and a side dish of hot corn-on-the-cob dripping in butter. And who could turn down a piece of pecan pie with a dip of vanilla ice cream or maybe just a plain ole peanut butter cookie. Well, so we like to eat, "high on the hog"; the recipes for that kind of "eatin" are right here in this cookbook. Remember one thing, if you haven't eaten fried okra, you haven't lived!

You know, I've actually heard that some people say that Texans like to brag, but that's just not true! Now look at the facts. What other state is bigger (forget Alaska, it's a newcomer)? What other state has a seashore, mountains, prairies, rivers, lakes, islands, piney woods, sand dunes and forests? Think of the bountiful fruits and vegetables grown year round in the valley and everybody deserves a tour of the Alamo once in a lifetime. Our panhandle of Texas has vast acreages of plowed red earth, farms of crop-textured fields, grazing cows and windswept prairies. Then there's the Big Bend country with canyons to hike, Indian trails to follow and a place to breath clean air that is crisp and cool. And remember the East Texas oil fields nestled among the stately pine trees with the dogwood blooming in the spring. And even West Texas has a beauty in its vast acres of wheat blowing in the wind, cattle grazing on elegant ranches that stretch as far as you can see. If you want "metropolitan", we've got Dallas and Houston with their industry and business centers. Well, shall I go on -- all the good things said about Texas are true so we don't have to brag! There's a fierce pride and loyalty in the Lone Star state that is recognized around the world. "Lesser mortals are pitied for the misfortune of not being born a Texan."

In my western boots, my ultra-suede suit and my 10 gallon hat, I stand proud to be a Texan and I say, "Enjoy this cookbook, *Black-Eyed Peas To Pralines* and thanks for purchasing it!"

Table of Contents

Black-Eyed Peas

Black-Eyed Pea Dip

3 (15 ounce) cans Jalapeño
   black-eyed peas
2 sticks margarine
2 cups grated sharp Cheddar
   cheese

1/2 onion, finely minced
1 teaspoon garlic powder
1 (4 ounce) can chopped green
   chilies

Drain peas and pour into blender or food processor. Blend; they do not need to be completely smooth. Set aside. In a large saucepan, on medium heat, melt margarine and cheese together. This will not mix completely smooth. Add onion, garlic powder, chopped green chilies and the blended black-eyed peas. Heat on medium heat, until warm, while stirring constantly. Serve hot in chafing dish with corn chips.

Black-Eyes and Rice Salad

1 (16 ounce) can Jalapeño
   black-eyed peas, rinsed
   and drained
1-1/2 cups cooked rice
1 (4 ounce) can sliced carrots,
   drained
2 stalks celery, sliced

1/2 purple onion, chopped
2/3 cup mayonnaise
1 tablespoon lemon juice
1/2 teaspoon dillweed
1/2 teaspoon garlic powder
1/2 teaspoon salt
1/2 teaspoon black pepper

In a mixing bowl, combine peas, rice, carrots, celery and onion; blend. Add the mayonnaise, lemon juice and seasonings and toss gently. Refrigerate. Serves 8.

Mexi-Pea Salad

1 pound lean ground meat
1/2 onion, chopped
1/2 cup chopped bell pepper
1 tablespoon chili powder
1/2 teaspoon salt
1/4 teaspoon pepper
1/2 head lettuce
2 tomatoes
1 cup grated Cheddar cheese

1 (15 ounce) can Jalapeño
   black-eyed peas, drained
1 (8-ounce) can whole kernel
   corn, drained
1 (7 ounce) package tortilla
   chips, lightly crushed
1 (8 ounce) bottle Catalina
   dressing

In a skillet, cook ground meat, onion and bell pepper until tender. Drain off any fat. Stir in chili powder, salt and pepper. Let cool. When ready to serve, combine meat mixture and remaining ingredients. Toss and serve immediately. Serves 15.

Marinated Black-Eyed Pea Salad

2 cans Jalapeño black-eyed
   peas, rinsed, drained
1 cup chopped celery
1 (4 ounce) can chopped green
   chilies
1/2 purple onion, chopped
2 tablespoons fresh cilantro*
2 cloves garlic, crushed

1 teaspoon seasoned salt
1/2 teaspoon black pepper
1 teaspoon Worcestershire
1-1/2 cups Italian dressing
2 hard boiled eggs, sliced
3 fresh green onions, tops too,
   chopped

In a large bowl, with a lid, combine all ingredients except eggs and green onions. Add the dressing and stir to mix well. If liquid doesn't cover peas, add a little more dressing. Marinate, covered for 24 hours in refrigerator. When ready to serve, use a slotted spoon and place salad in a crystal bowl. Sprinkle with sliced eggs and green onions. Serves 8 to 10. *You can substitute 2 teaspoons dried cilantro.

Lone Star Caviar

3 (16 ounce) cans black-eyed
   peas, rinsed and drained
1 (4 ounce) can chopped green
   chilies, drained
1 (2 ounce) jar pimiento,
   drained
1/2 purple onion, sliced
1 cup chopped celery

1 red bell pepper, chopped
Dressing:
2/3 cup vinegar
2/3 cup sugar
1/2 cup oil
1 teaspoon seasoned salt
1/2 teaspoon black pepper
1 pod garlic, minced

Drain peas, green chilies and pimiento. Place in container with a lid. Add onion, celery and bell pepper. In a small bowl, mix together all dressing ingredients and pour over vegetables. Refrigerate 24 hours before serving. Serves 10 as a salad.

Black-Eyed Pea Supper Casserole

1 pound ground beef
1 tablespoon oil
2/3 cup cornmeal
1/2 cup flour
1 teaspoon salt
1/2 teaspoon baking soda
1 cup buttermilk
2 eggs
1 stick margarine, melted

1 cup chopped onion
1 (15 ounce) can Jalapeño
   black-eyed peas, undrained
3/4 cup creamed corn
1-1/2 cups grated Cheddar
   cheese
Topping:
1 cup grated Cheddar cheese
Thick Chunky Salsa, optional

In a skillet, brown the beef in oil; drain any fat off. In a large mixing bowl combine the beef and all remaining ingredients except topping. Pour into a 3 quart buttered casserole and bake at 350 degrees for 45 minutes. Remove from oven and sprinkle remaining 1 cup grated cheese and return to oven for 5 minutes. When serving, place the Chunky Salsa in a gravy boat and serve it individually. Serve this casserole with a salad and you have "supper."

Lucky Black-Eyes

2 (10 ounce) packages frozen
   black-eyed peas (or fresh
   if you can get them)
1/3 cup chopped Jalapeño
   pepper (optional)
1 onion, chopped
Water

3 tablespoons bacon drippings
1 teaspoon salt
1 teaspoon pepper
1/2 teaspoon garlic powder
2 tablespoons Worcestershire
3/4 pound sausage, crumbled

In a large saucepan, combine peas, Jalapeño and onion; cover with water about 1 inch above the peas. Add bacon drippings, salt, pepper, garlic and Worcestershire. Bring to a boil and cook about 45 minutes. Add crumbled sausage and cook another 20 to 25 minutes. Check during cooking process to see if more water is needed. Serve with cornbread. Serves 8.

Good Fortune Black-Eyed Peas

1 pound dried black-eyed peas
2 quarts water
1/2 pound salt pork
1/2 onion, chopped

1 tablespoon chopped
   Jalapeño pepper
2 teaspoons sugar
1 teaspoon salt
1/2 teaspoon black pepper

Place black-eyed peas in a large kettle and cover with water. Soak for several hours. Then add salt pork, onion, Jalapeño pepper, sugar, salt and black pepper. Heat to the boiling point; then turn heat down and simmer about 1 hour and 30 minutes or until peas are tender. Serves 8.

New Year's Black-Eyed Peas

1 pound dried black-eyed peas
Water
2 teaspoons instant beef flavor
   bouillon
3/4 pound ham, cubed
1 cup chopped celery

1 bell pepper, chopped
1 onion, chopped
2 teaspoons garlic powder
2 teaspoons thyme
1/8 teaspoon cayenne pepper
1/2 teaspoon salt

Place peas in a Dutch oven and cover with water at least 2 or 3 inches above the peas. Add remaining ingredients and cover. Bring to a boil; lower heat to simmer. Cook for 2 to 2-1/2 hours or until peas are tender. Serves 8 to 10.

Peas and Tomatoes

1 bell pepper, chopped
1 large onion, chopped
2 stalks celery, chopped
1/4 stick margarine
2 cans Jalapeño black-eyed
    peas

1 (14-1/2 ounce) can stewed
    tomatoes
1 teaspoon garlic powder
1/4 cup catsup
3 chicken bouillon cubes

Saute the bell pepper, onion and celery in the margarine (don't overcook — let them stay a little crispy.) Add remaining ingredients and simmer for about 10 minutes. Good served with cornbread. Serves 8 to 10.

Hoppin' John

1 cup dried black-eyed peas
3-1/2 cups water
1/4 pound lean salt pork
1 green pepper, chopped
1 onion, chopped

1/2 teaspoon crushed red
    pepper
1/2 teaspoon black pepper
1/2 cup uncooked rice

Heat peas and water to boiling in a medium kettle. Boil uncovered for 2 minutes; remove from heat. Cover and let stand 1 hour. Cut salt pork in 8 pieces. Add salt pork, green pepper, onion, red pepper and black pepper and heat to boiling. Reduce heat, cover and simmer for 1 hour. Add rice and continue cooking for another 40 to 45 minutes stirring occasionally until rice is tender. Stir in additional water if necessary. Serves 6.

Hopping John Supper

2 cups dried black-eyed peas
3 tablespoons bacon drippings
1 teaspoon salt
1/2 teaspoon garlic powder
1 onion, chopped

1 bell pepper, chopped
1 pound sausage, crumbled,
    cooked, drained
1-1/2 cups cooked white rice

Place dried black-eyed peas, bacon drippings and seasonings in a large saucepan and cover with water. Bring to a boil and cook about 1 hour and 30 minutes or until peas are tender. When peas have cooked, place onion, bell pepper and sausage in a skillet and brown. Pour sausage and vegetables into saucepan with peas. Add rice. Heat and serve.

Appetizers

Texas Dip

1 pound lean ground beef

1 (8 ounce) package cream
   cheese, cut in cubes
1 cup hot picante sauce

In a large skillet, brown ground beef. Drain off any fat. Turn heat to low and place the cream cheese in skillet with the meat. Stirring constantly, cook until cream cheese has melted. Add picante sauce and blend well. Serve hot with chips. This can be used instead of melted cheese for nachos.

Prairie Fire

1 (16 ounce) can Refried Beans
1 stick margarine
2-1/2 cups shredded Cheddar
   cheese
1 (4 ounce) can chopped green
   chilies

1/2 onion, finely minced
3/4 teaspoon powdered garlic
1/2 teaspoon salt
1/4 teaspoon cayenne pepper

Combine beans, margarine and cheese in the top of a double boiler and heat slowly until the cheese is melted. Add remaining ingredients and mix well. Serve hot in chafing dish with chips or crackers.

Great Balls of Fire

1 pound hot sausage
1 can Rotel tomatoes and
   green chilies

1 pound Velveeta cheese

Brown sausage and drain off fat. Add tomatoes and green chilies; cut cheese in chunks and add to sausage mixture and melt. Serve in chafing dish with large corn chips. Also good over baked potatoes.

Quick Tuna Dip

1 (7 ounce) can white meat
   tuna, drained, separated
   with fork
1 (1.25 ounce) envelope onion
   soup mix

1 cup sour cream
1/3 cup finely chopped pecans
1/8 teaspoon cayenne pepper

Combine all ingredients and mix well. Chill several hours before serving. Serve with crackers.

For a quick dip for raw vegetables, combine 2 teaspoons curry powder, a pinch of ginger and 1 teaspoon lime juice to 1 cup mayonnaise. Refrigerate overnight.

Deviled Cheese Dip

1 (8 ounce) package cream
    cheese, softened
1 (2 ounce) jar pimentos,
    drained
1/4 teaspoon Worcestershire

1/2 cup mayonnaise
1 (3 ounce) can deviled ham
2 teaspoons minced onion
1 teaspoon curry powder

Put all ingredients in a food processor or blender and mix well. Refrigerate several hours before serving. Serve with chips or crackers. This is also good as a spread for ham sandwiches.

Smoked Oyster Dip

1 (8 ounce) package cream
    cheese, softened
1 cup mayonnaise
5 drops Tabasco
1 tablespoon lemon juice
1 tablespoon minced onion

1 (4-1/2 ounce) can black
    olives, chopped
1 (3-1/2 ounce) can smoked
    oysters, drained and finely
    chopped

Combine first 5 ingredients and mix well. Stir in olives and oysters. Serve with raw vegetables or crackers.

Cucumber Dip

1 (8 ounce) package cream
    cheese, softened
1 package Hidden Valley
    Ranch Dressing mix
1-1/2 cucumbers, peeled,
    grated (scoop out seeds)

1/4 cup mayonnaise
1 teaspoon lemon juice
1/2 cup finely chopped pecans
1/2 teaspoon salt
1/4 teaspoon garlic powder

Combine all ingredients and refrigerate. Serve with chips.

Place chilled butter or cream cheese in a microwave safe plate in the microwave oven for 10 to 15 seconds on high power to soften sufficiently for immediate use.

Curried Shrimp Dip

2-1/2 cups shrimp, peeled,
   deveined, chopped
1 can cream of shrimp soup,
   undiluted
1 (8 ounce) package cream
   cheese, softened
1/3 teaspoon curry powder

2 teaspoons lemon juice
1/4 teaspoon garlic powder
1/4 teaspoon salt
1/4 teaspoon white pepper
1 (4 ounce) can chopped ripe
   olives

In a mixing bowl, combine all ingredients except olives. Beat on medium speed 2 to 3 minutes. Add ripe olives and stir. Refrigerate. Serve with chips or crackers.

Shrimp Dip

3 cups cooked, deveined
   shrimp, finely chopped
2 tablespoons lemon juice
2 tablespoons horseradish

1/4 cup chili sauce
2/3 cup mayonnaise
1/2 teaspoon salt
1/2 teaspoon white pepper

Combine all ingredients and refrigerate. (If shrimp have been frozen, be sure to drain well.) Serve with cucumber or zucchini slices.

Speedy Shrimp Dip

1 (1/2 ounce) package green
   onion dip mix
1 cup sour cream

2 cups small frozen or canned
   shrimp, chopped
Paprika

Mix together onion dip mix and sour cream; blend. Add chopped shrimp. Chill several hours to combine flavors. When ready to serve, sprinkle paprika over dip. Serve with chips.

Cocktail Sauce for Shrimp

2 cups catsup
1/4 cup finely minced celery
1/2 cup fresh parsley
1/4 cup Worcestershire sauce

1/4 cup lemon juice
1/4 cup prepared horseradish
1/4 teaspoon sugar
Several drops Tabasco

Combine all ingredients; cover and chill. Makes enough sauce for 4 pounds cooked shrimp.

Tejas Sausage Dip

1 pound hot sausage
1 pound ground beef
1 chopped onion

1 can Rotel tomatoes and
   chilies
2 pounds Velveeta cheese
1 can cream of mushroom soup

Brown sausage, ground beef and onion and drain off grease. Add tomatoes and chilies; then cut Velveeta into chunks and add to meat mixture. Cook on low heat until cheese melts. Add undiluted soup and mix well. Serve hot.

Avocado Dip

3 (8 ounce) packages cream
   cheese, softened
4 avocados, peeled and
   mashed (save 1 seed)
3 tablespoons lemon juice

2 tablespoons mayonnaise
1/2 onion, very finely grated
1/2 teaspoon garlic powder
1 teaspoon salt
1 teaspoon Tabasco

In a mixing bowl, beat cream cheese with the electric mixer until smooth. Add remaining ingredients and beat until texture is smooth. Place in a "dip" container and place avocado seed in center until ready to serve (to prevent dip from turning brown). Refrigerate. Serve with chips.

Corn and Walnut Dip

2 (8 ounce) packages cream
   cheese, softened
1/4 cup fresh lime juice
1 tablespoon cumin
1 teaspoon salt
1 teaspoon pepper
1 teaspoon cayenne pepper

1 (8 ounce) can whole kernel
   corn, drained
1 cup chopped walnuts
1 (4 ounce) can chopped green
   chilies
3 green onions, chopped (tops
   too)

Whip the cream cheese until fluffy and beat in lime juice, cumin, salt, pepper and cayenne pepper until smooth. Stir in corn, walnuts, green chilies and onions. Refrigerate. Make at least 8 hours before serving. Serve with tortilla chips.

Marinate fresh pineapple strips in Grand Marnier for appetizer.

Crab Dip

1 (3 ounce) package cream
  cheese, softened
1/4 cup sour cream
1/4 cup mayonnaise
1 (6 ounce) can crab meat,
  drained and flaked

1 tablespoon finely grated
  onion
2 hard boiled eggs, mashed
1 teaspoon parsley flakes
1 tablespoon lemon juice
1/4 teaspoon celery salt
1/4 teaspoon Tabasco

In a medium mixing bowl, combine cream cheese, sour cream and mayonnaise. Blend until smooth. Add remaining ingredients and mix well. Refrigerate. Serve with chips or vegetable sticks.

Enchilada Dip

1 tablespoon oil
1/2 onion, chopped
1 pound lean ground beef
1 teaspoon garlic powder
1 can Mild Old El Paso
  Enchilada sauce

1 package dry enchilada sauce
1/2 cup tomato sauce
1/2 cup water
1 pound Jalapeño Velveeta
  cheese

In a large skillet, using the oil, saute onion and brown ground meat at the same time. With the heat still on, add garlic powder, can of enchilada sauce, package of enchilada sauce, tomato sauce and water. Let this simmer about 5 minutes or until water has cooked out. Cut Velveeta cheese into chunks and add to meat mixture. Stirring constantly, leave on medium heat until cheese has melted. Serve in a chafing dish with chips.

Deviled Egg Dip or Spread

3 hard cooked eggs, mashed
1 (3 ounce) package cream
  cheese, softened
1 cup grated Monterey Jack
  cheese
1/3 cup finely chopped pecans

1/4 cup mayonnaise
1/2 teaspoon prepared mustard
1/4 teaspoon salt
1/2 teaspoon white pepper
1/2 (4 ounce) can chopped
  green chilies

In a bowl, combine eggs and cream cheese and mix well. Add remaining ingredients and refrigerate. Serve as a dip with chips or as a spread on crackers.

Texas Crabgrass

3/4 stick margarine
1 medium onion, very finely
    chopped
2 (8 ounce) packages cream
    cheese, softened
1 (10 ounce) package frozen
    spinach, cooked and
    drained

1 (7 ounce) can crabmeat,
    drained
1/2 cup Parmesan cheese
1/2 teaspoon black pepper
1/4 teaspoon cayenne pepper
1/2 teaspoon salt
Melba rounds

In a saucepan, place margarine, onion and cream cheese and put on low to medium heat, stirring constantly, until margarine and cream cheese are well melted and mixed. (When draining spinach, use plenty paper towels to thoroughly blot all the water off the spinach.) Add spinach, crabmeat, cheese, black pepper, cayenne and salt. Place back on burner to warm the dip. Serve in a chafing dish, warm, with Melba rounds.

Cucumber Appetizers

3 cucumbers
1 (8 ounce) package cream
    cheese, softened
1 tablespoon mayonnaise
1/2 teaspoon garlic powder

1/2 teaspoon salt
1 tablespoon dried parsley
    flakes
1/4 cup stuffed green olives,
    chopped, well drained

Peel cucumbers and slice in half lengthwise. With a spoon or a scoop, remove seed making a rounded indention. Mix together remaining ingredients except olives. Whip until smooth and add olives; mix. Fill hollows with cream cheese mixture and press halves together. Wrap tightly in plastic wrap; chill. When ready to serve, cut crosswise in 1/2 inch slices. Serve on a relish tray.

Olive Cheese Appetizers

1 cup pimento-stuffed olives,
    chopped
3 green onions, finely chopped
3/4 cup Monterey Jack cheese,
    shredded
3/4 cup Cheddar cheese,
    shredded

1/2 cup mayonnaise
1/2 teaspoon chili powder
1/4 teaspoon salt
Several dashes of Tabasco
1 package English muffins

Combine all ingredients and mix well. Spread on English muffins and bake at 400 degrees until bubbly. Cut muffins into quarters and serve hot.

Too Easy To Be A Recipe — But Great
(Dip)

2 (8 ounce) packages cream
    cheese, softened

1 (16 ounce) jar Pace Thick and
    Chunky Medium Salsa

In a shallow bowl, mash cream cheese with a fork until you have it all messed up! Then add the salsa and mix all together with the fork so it will still be chunky. Serve with chips.

Celery Chunks

10 (4 inch) celery stalks
1 (5 ounce) jar Old English
    spread

1 (2-1/2 ounce) package thinly
    sliced corned beef*

Fill celery stalks with cheese. Wrap each filled stalk with a slice of the beef. Place seamside down on a dish. Refrigerate 2 hours and slice each stalk into 3 or 4 pieces. Serve on a relish tray. *Turkey slices would be good also.

Sweet 'N Sour Smokies

2 (5 ounce) packages tiny
    smokie link sausages

1 cup plum jam
1 cup prepared mustard

Place sausages in a 2 quart baking dish. In a saucepan, heat jam and mustard together and stir until well mixed. Pour over sausages and bake for one hour at 325 degrees. Serve warm with party picks.

Party Sausages

1 cup catsup
1 cup plum jelly
1 tablespoon lemon juice

4 tablespoon prepared mustard
2 (5 ounce) packages tiny
    smoked sausages*

In a saucepan, combine all ingredients except sausages and heat; mix well. Add sausages and simmer for 15 minutes. Serve with cocktail toothpicks. *You could substitute sliced weiners for the sausages.

Shrimp and Cheese Appetizers

1 pound cooked chopped
   shrimp
4 green onions, tops too,
   chopped
1/2 cup mayonnaise
1 cup grated Monterey Jack
   cheese

1/2 teaspoon instant chicken
   bouillon
1 tablespoon chopped
   pimentos
1 teaspoon Beau Monde
   seasoning
1 teaspoon dill weed
1 package English muffins

Combine all ingredients except muffins. Mix well. Spread on tops and bottoms of the split muffins and bake at 400 degrees for about 10 minutes or until bubbly. Slice in quarters and serve hot.

Sausage Pinwheels

2 cups flour
1/2 teaspoon salt
3 teaspoons baking powder
5 tablespoons shortening

2/3 cup milk
1 pound hot sausage, room
   temperature

In a mixing bowl, blend together flour, salt, baking powder, shortening and milk. Mix well. Divide dough into 3 parts. Roll each piece of dough into a thin rectangle. Divide sausage into thirds. Crumble sausage with fingers and spread on the 3 pieces of dough; pat sausage down on dough. Roll up like a jelly roll. Cover with foil and refrigerate overnight. When ready to serve, slice in thin slices and bake at 400 degrees for 15 to 20 minutes.

Cheese Puffs

2 cups sharp Cheddar cheese,
   shredded
1 stick margarine, very soft
1/2 teaspoon salt

1 teaspoon paprika
1/2 teaspoon garlic powder
1 cup flour
48 green stuffed olives

In a large mixing bowl, mix cheese and margarine. Stir in dry ingredients and mix well. Wrap a teaspoon of mixture around each olive and place on cookie sheet. Bake at 375 degrees for 15 to 16 minutes.

Lemons will yield more juice when slightly warm. You can microwave a lemon for 2 minutes on low power.

Savory Chicken Wings

20 to 25 chicken wings
3/4 cup water
1 cup soy sauce
1 cup sugar
1/4 cup oil

1/4 cup orange juice
1 teaspoon savory
1 teaspoon garlic powder
1 teaspoon ground ginger
1/2 teaspoon pepper

Cut off and discard tips of wings. Separate the other 2 parts of the wings and place in a container with a lid. Mix remaining ingredients and pour over the wings. Cover and refrigerate overnight. When ready to cook, place wings in a shallow baking dish and pour only 1-1/2 cups of the marinade over wings. Bake, uncovered at 325 degrees for 1 hour and 30 minutes. Turn several times during baking.

Texas Party Mix

1 (12 ounce) box corn Chex
1 (12 ounce) box wheat Chex
1 (12 ounce) box Crispix
1 package thin pretzels
2 cans mixed nuts
2 cans peanuts
2-1/2 sticks margarine

2 tablespoons Lowry's
    seasoned salt
2 tablespoons garlic powder
2 tablespoons Tabasco
2 tablespoons Worcestershire
2 teaspoons cayenne pepper

Mix first 6 ingredients together in a large roasting pan. Melt margarine and add next 5 ingredients and pour over cereal mixture and stir. Bake at 250 degrees for about 2 hours. Store in air-tight containers.

Marinated Shrimp

2 pounds cooked shrimp
1 onion, thinly sliced into rings
1/2 cup chopped celery
1 cup oil
3/4 cup white vinegar
1 teaspoon sugar
1/4 cup capers with juice
2 teaspoons celery salt

1 teaspoon parsley
1 clove garlic, crushed
1-1/2 tablespoons whole cloves
1 teaspoon seasoned salt
1/2 black pepper
1/4 teaspoon Tabasco
5 bay leaves

If shrimp are large, slice lengthwise. Make alternate layers of shrimp and onion in a sealable container. Mix remaining ingredients and pour over shrimp and onion. Cover and refrigerate for 24 hours before serving. Shake container occasionally. When ready to serve, remove shrimp and onion from marinade and place in a glass bowl. Serve with cocktail picks.

Chili Cheese Log

1 (8 ounce) package cream
  cheese, softened
2 cups shredded Cheddar
  cheese, softened
2 tablespoons mayonnaise

1 tablespoon lemon juice
1/2 teaspoon garlic powder
1/2 cup finely chopped pecans
1 teaspoon chili powder
1 teaspoon paprika

In a mixing bowl, combine cheeses, mayonnaise, lemon juice and garlic powder. Beat with mixer until well blended. Stir in pecans. Shape into a roll about 1-1/2 inches in diameter. Mix together the chili powder and paprika and sprinkle roll with mixture. Roll up cheese log in wax paper and refrigerate. Serve with crackers.

Spicy Pecans

1/2 stick margarine
2 tablespoons Worcestershire
1 teaspoon salt
1/2 teaspoon cinnamon
1/8 teaspoon cloves

1/4 teaspoon garlic powder
1/4 teaspoon cayenne
1/4 teaspoon Tabasco
4 cups pecan halves

Melt margarine in heavy skillet and stir in remaining ingredients, except pecans. Mix well and add pecans stirring until pecans are well coated. Place in a single layer in an ungreased jelly roll pan. Toast pecans at 300 degrees for 25 to 30 minutes. Stir frequently.

Delicious Dip for Strawberries

1 jar marshmallow cream
1 (8 ounce) tub soft cream
  cheese, room temperature

Dash of cinnamon
Fresh Strawberries*

Combine marshmallow cream, cream cheese and cinnamon. Beat until smooth. Serve with a big bowl of cool, fresh strawberries. *Good with other fruit too.

3 tablespoons bottled juice will substitute for juice of 1 lemon.

Breads

Apricot Bread

1 cup finely chopped, dried
   apricots
1/2 cup boiling water
1-1/3 cups sugar
1/4 stick margarine, softened
2 cups flour

2 teaspoons baking powder
1/2 teaspoon soda
1/2 teaspoon salt
1 egg
1/2 cup orange juice
1 cup chopped pecans

Place apricots in mixing bowl, pour in boiling water and let soak for 30 minutes. Add remaining ingredients except pecans and mix well. Stir in pecans. Pour into a greased and floured loaf pan. Let rise for 15 minutes. Bake at 325 degrees for one hour and 10 minutes or until toothpick comes out clean. Cool on a wire rack.

Apple Banana Bread

3 apples, peeled, grated
3 bananas, mashed
2 teaspoons lemon juice
1 stick margarine, softened
2 cups sugar
2 eggs

3 cups flour
1-1/2 teaspoons baking powder
1-1/2 teaspoons baking soda
1/2 teaspoon salt
1 teaspoon vanilla

Sprinkle apples and bananas with lemon juice. In a mixing bowl, cream together margarine, sugar and eggs and beat well. Stir in fruit. Add dry ingredients and vanilla. Stir. Pour into 2 greased and floured loaf pans. Bake at 350 degrees for 50 to 55 minutes or until golden brown.

For a fun breakfast for the kids, cut canned biscuits in quarters and drop them in hot oil and fry until brown. Roll the warm biscuit pieces in a cinnamon-sugar mixture before serving.

Poppyseed Swiss Bread

3-1/2 cups flour
1-1/2 tablespoons baking
    powder
1/2 teaspoon salt
1 tablespoon sugar
1/3 cup margarine

2 cups grated Swiss cheese
2 tablespoons poppyseed
2 eggs
1-1/2 cups milk
2 teaspoons prepared mustard

In a mixing bowl, combine first 4 ingredients and cut in margarine until mixture resembles coarse meal. Stir in cheese and poppyseed. Then add eggs, milk and mustard, stirring just until moistened. Spoon batter into 2 greased and floured 9x5x3 inch loaf pans. Bake at 350 degrees for 1 hour and 10 minutes or until a toothpick inserted in center comes out clean. Cool bread in pan for 10 minutes; then remove from pan. Delicious toasted with a little butter on bread.

Applesauce Bread

2 cups flour
1 cup sugar
1 teaspoon baking powder
1 teaspoon soda
1 teaspoon salt
1-1/2 teaspoons cinnamon
1/2 teaspoon nutmeg

1-1/2 teaspoons lemon peel
1 teaspoon vanilla
1 stick margarine, softened
1 cup applesauce
2 eggs
1/2 cup chopped pecans

In a large mixing bowl, combine all ingredients except the pecans and beat at medium speed until well blended. Stir in the pecans and pour into a loaf pan which has been greased and floured. Bake at 350 degrees for 55 to 60 minutes. Test with toothpick for doneness. Cool before slicing.

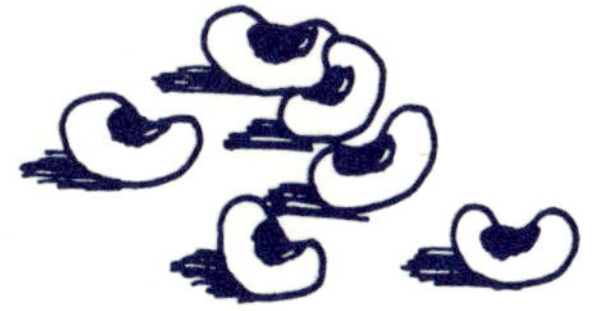

*Use softened cream chese as filling on
fruit bread.*

Just Plain Ole Cornbread

1 cup flour
1 cup yellow cornmeal
1/4 cup sugar
4 teaspoons baking powder
3/4 teaspoon salt
2 eggs
1 cup milk
1/4 cup oil

Mix all ingredients together; blend well. Pour into a greased 9 x 13 inch baking pan. Bake at 350 degrees for 30 minutes or until lightly browned.

Jalapeño Cornbread

2-1/2 cups yellow cornmeal
1 cup flour
2 tablespoons sugar
1 tablespoon salt
4 teaspoons baking powder
3 eggs, room temperature
1/2 cup oil
1-1/2 cups buttermilk
1 (15 ounce) can cream-style
   corn
6 to 8 Jalapeño peppers,
   chopped
1/4 cup chopped bell pepper
2 cups grated sharp Cheddar
   cheese
1 onion, finely chopped
3 slices bacon, cooked and
   crumbled

Stir dry ingredients together and add eggs, oil and buttermilk; mix well. Stir in the creamed corn, Jalapeños, bell peppers, cheese, onion and bacon; mix well. Pour into a 9 x 13 inch greased baking dish and bake at 375 degrees for 45 minutes or until lightly browned.

Tex-Mex Cornbread

3 cups yellow cornmeal
1/3 cup flour
3 teaspoons baking powder
1 teaspoon salt
2 tablespoons sugar
2-1/2 cups milk
1/2 cup oil or bacon drippings
3 eggs, beaten
1 cup chopped onion
1 cup cream-style cooked corn
1/4 to 1/2 cup finely chopped
   canned Jalapeño peppers
1-1/2 cups grated Cheddar
   cheese

In a large mixing bowl, combine cornmeal, flour, baking powder, salt and sugar. Add milk, oil or bacon drippings and beaten eggs and mix until smooth. Stir in onion, corn, Jalapeños and cheese. Pour into a well-greased 9 x 13 inch baking pan and bake at 400 degrees for 35 minutes or until lightly browned.

Spicy Cornbread Twists

1/3 stick margarine
1/3 cup cornmeal
1/4 teaspoon red pepper

1 (11 ounce) can refrigerated
soft breadsticks

Place margarine in a pie plate and melt the margarine in the oven. Remove from oven. On a piece of wax paper, mix cornmeal and red pepper. Roll breadsticks in margarine and then in cornmeal mixture. Twist the breadsticks as label directs and place on a large cookie sheet. Bake at 350 degrees 15 to 18 minutes. Makes 8 breadsticks.

Squash Cornbread

1 cup yellow cornmeal
1 cup flour
2 tablespoons light brown
    sugar
5 teaspoons baking powder
1 teaspoon salt
1/2 teaspoon ground cumin
1 tablespoon dried parsley
    flakes

3 dashes cayenne pepper
1 grated zucchini or yellow
    squash (about 1 cup)
2 eggs
1 cup milk
1/4 cup oil
3/4 cup grated Cheddar cheese
1 (4 ounce) can chopped green
    chilies

In a large bowl, mix together cornmeal, flour, brown sugar, baking powder, salt, cumin, parsley and cayenne pepper. Add the squash, eggs, milk, oil, cheese and green chilies. Mix well. Pour into a greased 9 x 13 inch baking pan. Cook at 400 degrees for 25 to 30 minutes or until lightly browned. Serves 8 to 10.

Cheese Corn Muffins

3/4 cup flour
2 teaspoons baking powder
1/2 teaspoon salt
2 tablespoons sugar
1/2 cup yellow cornmeal

1 cup grated Cheddar cheese
1 egg
3/4 cup milk
1/3 stick margarine, melted

In a bowl, combine flour, baking powder, salt, sugar, cornmeal and cheese; mix. Make a well in the center and add the egg, milk and margarine. Stir just to moisten. Grease 12 muffin tins and pour batter in muffin tins. Bake at 400 degrees for about 20 minutes or until golden brown.

Beer Bread

3 cups biscuit mix
1/4 cup sugar

1 can beer
1/2 stick margarine, melted

Combine biscuit mix and sugar in bowl. Add beer and mix just until blended. Pour into a greased and floured loaf pan. Let rise 10 minutes. Bake at 350 degrees for 40 to 50 minutes. While bread is still in pan, pour melted margarine over bread and let stand 10 minutes. Turn bread out on rack. Serve hot or make ahead of time, wrap in foil and warm in oven. Also very good toasted.

Sesame Toast

2 tablespoons sesame seeds
2 tablespoons margarine
1 stick margarine
1/4 teaspoon basil

1/2 teaspoon rosemary
1/4 teaspoon marjoram
1/2 teaspoon garlic powder
1/2 loaf French bread

In a medium saucepan, brown sesame seeds in 2 tablespoons margarine. Add stick of margarine; melt and add seasonings. Let stand overnight in refrigerator. When ready to make toast, stir the margarine mixture and spread mixture on bread slices. Bake at 300 degrees for 20 minutes or until slightly browned.

Banana Muffins

1 cup Bran Flakes
1/4 cup milk
2 medium bananas, mashed
    (about 1 cup)
1/3 cup oil
1 cup flour

2 teaspoons baking powder
1/4 teaspoon baking soda
1/2 teaspoon salt
2/3 cup sugar
1 egg

In a mixing bowl, combine the Bran Flakes, milk, bananas and oil; mix. Sift together dry ingredients and add to banana mixture; mix. Add sugar and egg, mixing only until all is combined. Fill 12 greased, large size muffin cups. Bake at 400 degrees about 16 to 20 minutes.

Orange Pecan Muffins

2/3 cup sugar
1/2 cup orange juice
1 teaspoon grated orange rind
1 egg, lightly beaten

3 tablespoons oil
2 cups biscuit mix
1/2 cup orange marmalade
1/2 cup chopped pecans

In a mixing bowl, combine the sugar, orange juice, orange rind, egg and oil and mix well. Add the biscuit mix and beat vigorously for 30 seconds. Stir in the marmalade and pecans and pour into 12 buttered, large-size muffin tins. Bake at 400 degrees for 20 minutes or until lightly browned.

Always cut fresh breads with a hot knife.

Maple Muffins

1-1/2 cups flour
1/3 cup sugar
1 tablespoon baking powder
1/2 teaspoon salt
1/4 cup shortening
3/4 cup oatmeal
1 egg, beaten
1/2 cup milk

1/2 cup maple syrup
3 or 4 drops of maple flavoring
 (optional)
Icing:
2 tablespoons margarine,
 softened
1/3 cup powdered sugar
2 tablespoons maple syrup

In a large mixing bowl, combine flour, sugar, baking powder and salt. Cut in shortening until mixture resembles coarse crumbs. Stir in oatmeal. Add egg, milk and syrup and stir only until dry ingredients are moistened. Fill greased muffin cups 2/3 full. Bake at 400 degrees for 18 to 20 minutes. Makes 12 muffins. Cool. For the icing, combine the margarine, powdered sugar and maple syrup. Mix until smooth. Ice muffins.

Apricot Pineapple Muffins

1 stick margarine, softened
3/4 cup brown sugar
1 egg
2/3 cup crushed pineapple
 with juice
1/3 cup dried apricots, very
 finely chopped

1 cup flour
1/2 teaspoon baking soda
1/2 teaspoon salt
1 cup quick rolled oats
(Cutting dried apricots with
 kitchen scissors is easier
 than chopping)

In a mixing bowl combine and mix the margarine, sugar, and egg. Add pineapple and apricots and mix. Combine all dry ingredients and add to pineapple and apricots and mix. Combine all dry ingredients and add to first mixture. Mix well. Spoon into well-greased muffin tins and bake at 350 degrees for 20 minutes. Makes 12 muffins or 36 miniature muffins.

For light and fluffy waffles, substitute club soda for the milk and add a little more oil.

Strawberry Coffee Cake

1 (8 ounce) package cream
   cheese, softened
1 stick margarine, softened
1 cup sugar
1/4 cup milk
2 eggs
1 teaspoon vanilla
2 cups flour

1 teaspoon baking powder
1/2 teaspoon baking soda
1 (18 ounce) jar strawberry
   preserves*
1/4 cup packed brown sugar
1/2 cup chopped pecans
1/2 stick margarine, melted

In a large mixing bowl, cream together the cream cheese, 1 stick margarine, sugar, milk, eggs and vanilla; beating well. Combine flour, baking powder and soda and blend with cream cheese mixture. Beat well. Batter will be stiff. Spread 1/2 batter in a 9 x 13 inch baking pan that has been greased and floured. Ice evenly with preserves and dot with remaining batter. Spread the batter out as evenly as possible. Mix the brown sugar and pecans together and sprinkle over top of cake; then drizzle with melted margarine. Bake at 350 degrees for 40 minutes. *Different kinds of preserves can also be used.

Good Morning Coffee Cake

2-1/3 cups flour
1-1/2 cups sugar
3/4 teaspoon salt
3/4 cup shortening
2 teaspoons baking powder
3/4 cup milk
2 eggs
1 teaspoon vanilla

1 (3 ounce) package cream
   cheese, softened
1 can Eagle brand condensed
   milk
1/3 cup lemon juice
1 can peach pie filling
2 teaspoons cinnamon
3/4 cup chopped pecans

In a mixing bowl, combine flour, sugar and salt; cut in shortening until crumbly. Reserve 1 cup crumb mixture. To remaining crumb mixture, add baking powder, milk, eggs and vanilla. Beat on medium speed for 2 minutes. Spread into a greased and floured 9 x 13 inch baking dish. Bake at 350 degrees for 25 minutes. In another bowl, beat cream cheese and condensed milk until fluffy; gradually fold in lemon juice, peach pie filling and cinnamon. Spoon this mixture over cake that has cooked 25 minutes. With the remaining crumb mixture, add pecans and sprinkle on top of cake. Bake 30 minutes longer. Serve warm.

Cherry-Nut Breakfast Cake

1 (8 ounce) package cream
    cheese
2 sticks margarine, softened
1-1/2 cups sugar
1-1/2 teaspoons vanilla
3 eggs
2-1/4 cups flour
1-1/2 teaspoons baking powder
1 (10 ounce) jar maraschino
    cherries, drained

1/2 cup chopped pecans
Glaze:
1-1/2 cups powdered sugar
2-1/2 tablespoons milk
2 tablespoons margarine,
    melted
1/2 teaspoon almond extract
1/2 cup chopped pecans

In a large mixing bowl, blend cream cheese, margarine, sugar, vanilla and eggs. Beat 3 minutes. Add flour and baking powder and beat well. Cut each cherry into 3 or 4 pieces; then fold in cherries and 1/2 cup chopped pecans. Pour batter into a greased and floured 9 x 13 inch baking pan and bake at 350 degrees for 40 minutes. Just before cake is done, mix together the powdered sugar, milk, melted margarine and almond extract. Glaze while cake is still warm. Top with remaining 1/2 cup pecans.

Apricot Coffee Cake

2 sticks margarine, softened
1 (3 ounce) package cream
    cheese
1-1/2 cups sugar
2 eggs
1 teaspoon vanilla
1-1/2 teaspoons baking powder
2-1/4 cups flour

1 can apricot pie filling*
Icing:
1-1/2 cups powdered sugar
2 tablespoons milk
2 tablespoons margarine,
    melted
1/2 teaspoon almond extract

In a mixing bowl combine the margarine, cream cheese and sugar; beat together at low speed. Add eggs and vanilla and beat together at medium speed. Add baking powder and flour and beat well. Spread 2/3 of the batter in a greased and floured 9 x 13 inch baking pan. Spread pie filling over batter. Using a teaspoon, drop remaining batter over pie filling. Bake at 350 degrees for 40 to 45 minutes. Cool. Mix powdered sugar, milk, margarine and almond extract together and beat until smooth. Drizzle icing over cake. *Other pie fillings may be used.

Salads

Crunchy Broccoli Salad

1 bunch fresh broccoli,
    washed and well drained
4 green onions, tops too,
    chopped
4 hard cooked eggs, sliced
1 (15 ounce) can sliced water
    chestnuts, drained

1 (14 ounce) can bean sprouts,
    drained
1 package Ranch Salad
    Dressing Mix
1 cup mayonnaise

Cut broccoli into small bite-size pieces and make sure the broccoli has dried out completely. (It is a good idea to wash and drain broccoli 1 day earlier and place in a plastic bag with a couple of paper towels to help soak up moisture.) Mix together the broccoli, onions, eggs, water chestnuts and bean sprouts in a large mixing bowl. In a small bowl mix Ranch Dressing with mayonnaise; add to broccoli mixture; toss. Refrigerate.

Broccoli Salad

1 bunch fresh broccoli, cut in
    small bite-sized florets
1/2 purple onion, sliced and
    separated
1/2 cup raisins
1 package slivered almonds
1/2 cup chopped celery

Imitation bacon bits
Dressing:
1 cup mayonnaise
1/4 cup sugar
2 tablespoons vinegar
1 teaspoon salt
1/2 teaspoon pepper

Make sure broccoli has been well drained. In a large bowl, combine broccoli, onion, raisins, almonds and celery. Mix together dressing ingredients and pour over vegetables; toss. Refrigerate several hours before serving. Sprinkle bacon bits over salad just before serving. Serves 6 to 8.

Add a little whipped cream to chicken or turkey salad to make it light and delicate.

Marinated Vegetable Salad

1 (16 ounce) can sliced carrots
1 bell pepper, cut in strips
2 onions, cut in rings
2 stalks celery, sliced
1-1/2 cups raw cauliflower , sliced
1 can condensed tomato soup

1 cup sugar
3/4 cup vinegar
1/3 cup oil
1/2 teaspoon Tabasco
1/2 teaspoon pepper
1 teaspoon prepared mustard
1/2 teaspoon salt

Combine all vegetables in a large bowl that has a lid. In a smaller bowl, mix together the soup, sugar, vinegar, oil, Tabasco, pepper, mustard and salt. Pour mixture over vegetables. Cover and chill at least 8 hours. Serves 8 to 10.

Sesame Spinach Salad

1/4 cup oil
2 tablespoons white wine vinegar
1 teaspoon sugar
2 tablespoons chopped parsley
1 teaspoon Beau Monde seasoning
1/4 teaspoon salt

1/2 teaspoon pepper
1/8 teaspoon garlic powder
1 pound fresh spinach
2 tablespoons sesame seeds, toasted
2 hard-boiled eggs, chopped
1 cup croutons

Combine the first 8 ingredients in a jar; cover tightly and shake vigorously. Remove stems from spinach; wash leaves thoroughly and pat dry. Tear into bite-size pieces. When ready to serve, combine spinach, sesame seeds and eggs in a bowl; add dressing and toss gently. Sprinkle with croutons. Serves 4 to 6.

It is easier to separate eggs when very cold ones are used.

Marinated Brussel Sprouts

2 (10 ounce) packages frozen
  Brussel sprouts
1/2 cup oil
1/2 cup tarragon vinegar
2 tablespoons sugar

1 clove garlic, crushed
1 teaspoon salt
1/2 teaspoon seasoned salt
1 teaspoon pepper
2 small onions, cut in rings

Cook Brussel sprouts according to instructions on package. *For quicker cooking, you can pierce the boxes several times and cook in the microwave on high for 6 to 7 minutes for each box. In a medium size container with a lid, mix the oil, vinegar, sugar, garlic, salt, seasoned salt and pepper. Add Brussel sprouts and onion rings to the dressing. Put lid on container and shake well. Refrigerate at least 24 hours before serving.

Fresh Vegetable Salad

2 carrots, grated
1/2 purple onion, thinly sliced
  and separated
1 bell pepper, cut in thin strips
4 small yellow squash, thinly
  sliced
3 small zucchini, thinly sliced
6 radishes, thinly sliced
2 stalks celery, thinly sliced
1/2 bunch fresh broccoli, cut
  into small bite-size florets

Dressing:
1 tablespoon Lowry's
  seasoned salt
1 tablespoon parsley flakes
1 teaspoon black pepper
1/2 teaspoon garlic powder
1/2 cup red wine vinegar
1/2 cup oil
2 tablespoons sugar
1/2 cup mayonnaise

In a large bowl with a lid combine all salad ingredients. Mix together all dressing ingredients. Pour over vegetables and shake so dressing is well mixed with the vegetables. Refrigerate several hours before serving. Serves 8 to 10.

White pepper is stronger than black pepper.

Wagon Wheels

3 hard cooked eggs
1 (3 ounce) package cream
  cheese, softened
1 cup grated Monterey Jack
  cheese
1/3 cup very finely chopped
  celery
Several shakes Tabasco

1/3 cup finely chopped pecans
1/4 cup mayonnaise
1 teaspoon prepared mustard
1/4 teaspoon salt
1/4 teaspoon white pepper
3 medium green peppers
Lettuce leaves

Mash eggs and mix well with cream cheese and Monterey Jack cheese. Add celery, Tabasco, pecans, mayonnaise, mustard, salt and white pepper. Mix well. Cut off tops of green peppers and remove seeds and membranes. Stuff with the cheese mixture. Chill several hours or preferably overnight. Cut peppers in 1/4 inch rings. For each serving, overlap 3 pepper slices on a lettuce leaf. Serves 6 to 8.

Sprouts 'N Bean Salad

1/2 cup sugar
1/2 cup white vinegar
1/2 cup oil
3/4 teaspoon garlic powder
1 teaspoon seasoned salt
1/2 teaspoon pepper

2 (16 ounce) cans green beans
1 (16 ounce) can bean sprouts
1 (4 ounce) jar pimento,
  drained
1 package slivered almonds

Heat sugar, vinegar, oil, garlic powder, salt and pepper in a saucepan until sugar is dissolved. Mix green beans, bean sprouts, pimento and almonds in a bowl with a lid. Cover with sugar and vinegar mixture and marinate in refrigerator at least 8 hours before serving. Serves 8 to 10.

Cottage cheese will keep twice as long if carton is stored upside down.

Calico Salad

1 (16 ounce) can French style
    green beans
1 (16 ounce) can peas
1 (16 ounce) can whole kernel
    white corn
1 cup finely chopped celery
1 green pepper, chopped
1 bunch green onions, chopped
1 (2 ounce) jar chopped
    pimento, drained

Dressing:
1/2 cup sugar
1/2 cup wine vinegar
1/2 cup oil
1 teaspoon salt
1/2 teaspoon pepper
1/2 teaspoon tarragon
1/2 teaspoon basil

Drain all vegetables and combine in a bowl that has a lid. Mix dressing ingredients thoroughly and pour over vegetables. Cover and refrigerate overnight. Will keep several days in refrigerator. Serves 8 to 10.

Crunchy Spinach Salad

1 pound fresh spinach, torn
    into pieces
1 purple onion, chopped
1/2 (16 ounce) can bean
    sprouts, well drained
1 (8 ounce) can sliced water
    chestnuts, drained
3 hard boiled eggs, sliced

6 slices bacon, cooked and
    crumbled
Dressing:
1/2 cup oil
1/2 cup white vinegar
3 tablespoons ketchup
1/3 cup sugar
1 teaspoon salt
1/2 teaspoon pepper

In a large salad bowl, combine the spinach, onion, bean sprouts, water chestnuts and boiled eggs. Chill. Combine dressing ingredients in a jar with a lid and shake well. Refrigerate. When ready to serve, toss salad with the dressing and garnish with bacon.

Sour cream will keep longer in the refrigerator if stored upside down so that air cannot enter the carton.

Cauliflower Caesar Salad

1 head cauliflower, broken up,
   washed, well drained
1/2 bunch broccoli, washed,
   drained
1 cup chopped celery
4 green onions, tops too,
   chopped

6 ounces Monterey Jack
   cheese, cut in chunks
1 package Caesar salad
   dressing mix
1 cup mayonnaise

Break up and cut up cauliflower and broccoli into bite-size pieces. Make sure cauliflower and broccoli are well drained. Place cauliflower, broccoli, celery, onions and cheese in a bowl with a lid. In a small bowl, mix Caesar salad mix and mayonnaise. Add to cauliflower-broccoli mixture. Toss and refrigerate several hours for flavors to blend. Serves 8.

Summer Cucumber Crisps

1 pint white vinegar
1-1/2 cups sugar
1 clove garlic, chopped
1 tablespoon whole cloves
1 tablespoon whole allspice
2 bay leaves
2 sticks cinnamon

1 tablespoon whole celery seed
1 tablespoon mustard seed
1 tablespoon peppercorns
1 teaspoon powdered ginger
5 to 6 cucumbers, preferably
   fresh from the garden

In a medium saucepan combine all ingredients except the cucumbers. Boil 12 to 15 minutes. Cool mixture and strain. Thinly slice the cucumbers and place in a large jar or bowl with a lid. Add cooled marinade and cover tightly. Keep refrigerated.

Always cook eggs at a low to moderate temperature so as not to toughen them.

Cucumbers With Sour Cream

3 cucumbers
1 (8 ounce) carton sour cream
1/2 onion, very finely minced
2 tablespoons lemon juice
1 teaspoon salt
1 tablespoon sugar

Peel and slice cucumbers and place in covered dish. Combine remaining ingredients and pour over cucumbers. Refrigerate.

Spicy Green Bean Salad

2/3 cup oil
1/3 cup vinegar
1 teaspoon sugar
1 package spaghetti sauce mix
2 cans cut green beans, drained
5 fresh green onions, sliced
2 cups shredded lettuce
6 slices bacon, fried crisp and
　　broken up

In a bowl with a lid, combine the oil, vinegar, sugar and spaghetti sauce mix. Shake and mix well. Add the green beans and onions; mix and chill several hours. Just before serving, toss the green bean mixture with the lettuce and sprinkle the bacon pieces over top. Serves 8.

Waldorf Salad Supreme

1 tablespoon lemon juice
2 apples, coarsely chopped
1 cup chopped celery
1 (16 ounce) can pineapple
　　chunks, drained
1/2 cup pecan halves
2/3 cup mayonnaise
Lettuce

In a mixing bowl, pour lemon juice over apples and toss to spread lemon juice. Add all remaining ingredients except lettuce; toss. Serve on a lettuce leaf. Serves 6 to 8.

Keep onions in your refrigerator before you use them to cut down on the tears and strong odor when they are cut.

Asparagus Salad

2 (10 ounce) cans whole
   asparagus spears, drained
1/2 cup sour cream
1/3 cup mayonnaise

1/2 teaspoon seasoned pepper
2 tablespoons sesame seeds,
   lightly toasted

On a small platter (or individual salad plates) place asparagus in a row. In a small bowl, mix sour cream, mayonnaise and pepper. Spoon mayonnaise mixture down center of asparagus. Sprinkle sesame seeds on top of dressing. Serve immediately.

Asparagus Mold

1 package plain gelatin
1/4 cup water
1 (14-1/2 ounce) can all green
   asparagus
1 cup asparagus liquid
1/2 cup mayonnaise

1/2 cup sour cream
1 teaspoon salt
2 tablespoons lemon juice
1 cup chopped almonds,
   slightly toasted

Dissolve gelatin in 1/4 cup water. Heat asparagus liquid in a saucepan (add water to make 1 cup). Pour dissolved gelatin into heated liquid. Refrigerate until partially set. Add mayonnaise, sour cream, salt, lemon juice; mix. Cut asparagus up into smaller pieces; then fold in asparagus pieces and the almonds. Pour into 12 molds. Refrigerate several hours before serving.

Grape Toss

2 cups seedless green grapes,
   cut in half
1 (16 ounce) can pineapple
   chunks, drained

3/4 cup chopped pecans
2 (3 ounce) packages cream
   cheese, softened
1/4 cup mayonnaise

In a mixing bowl, combine grapes, pineapple and pecans. In a smaller bowl, mix together the cream cheese and mayonnaise and whip with a fork until fairly smooth. Add grape mixture and toss. Refrigerate. Serve on a lettuce leaf. Serves 6.

Put a little oil on your cheese grater before using to make clean-up easier

Emerald Salad

1 (3 ounce) package lime
  gelatin
3/4 cup boiling water
1-1/2 cucumbers, peeled and
  shredded (scoop seeds out)
2 teaspoons finely grated onion
1 tablespoon lemon juice

1/4 teaspoon salt
1 cup mayonnaise
1 cup cream style small curd
  cottage cheese
1 (2 ounce) package slivered
  almonds, toasted

Dissolve gelatin in water and cool slightly. (Make sure you have at least 1 full cup of cucumbers.) Add cucumber, onion, lemon juice, salt, mayonnaise, cottage cheese and almonds. Pour into individual molds or into a 9 inch glass dish. Chill 8 hours. Serves 8.

Orange Fluff Salad

1 (12 ounce) carton small curd
  cottage cheese
1 (3 ounce) package orange
  Jello
1 (11 ounce) can mandarin
  oranges, drained

1 (15 ounce) can crushed
  pineapple, drained
1/2 cup coconut
1/2 cup chopped pecans
1 (8 ounce) carton Cool Whip

In a large mixing bowl, combine cottage cheese and dry orange Jello and mix well. Stir in oranges, pineapple, coconut and pecans. Fold in Cool Whip. Refrigerate. Serve in a pretty crystal bowl.

If you don't have the canned water chestnuts called for in a salad recipe, try adding sliced radishes.

Cool Fruit Salad

1 can Eagle Brand condensed
   milk
1 can cherry pie filling*
1 (17 ounce) can pineapple
   chunks, well drained

1 (17 ounce) can fruit cocktail,
   well drained
1 cup chopped pecans
1 (8 ounce) carton Cool Whip

Mix condensed milk and pie filling in a large container. Add pineapple, fruit cocktail and pecans and blend. Fold in Cool Whip. Refrigerate. Serve in a pretty crystal bowl. Serves 10 to 12. *Other pie fillings can be used.

Peaches 'N Cream Salad

1 (6 ounce) package lemon
   gelatin
2 cups boiling water

1 (3 ounce) package cream
   cheese, softened
1 cup Cool Whip
1 can peach pie filling

In a mixing bowl, combine gelatin and boiling water. Mix well and pour half into a separate bowl and set aside. With the gelatin in mixing bowl, add the cream cheese and beat for 2 minutes. Place in refrigerator just until it begins to thicken but not set. Fold in Cool Whip and pour into a 9 x 13 inch glass dish. Refrigerate until set. With remaining gelatin, mix in the peach pie filling and pour over first layer. Refrigerate.

Your gelatin will come out of your mold easier if you grease the mold with a little bit of mayonnaise before you fill it.

Spicy Cranberry Salad

1 (6 ounce) package raspberry
   gelatin
1/4 teaspoon salt
1/4 teaspoon cinnamon
Dash cloves

1-3/4 cup boiling water
2 cans whole cranberry sauce
1 apple
1 can mandarin oranges,
   drained

Place gelatin, salt, cinnamon and cloves in a large mixing bowl and pour boiling water over gelatin. Mix until gelatin is well dissolved. Add both cans cranberry sauce and place in refrigerator until mixture begins to thicken. Peel and grate apple and hurriedly add to gelatin mixture so apple won't darken. Add oranges and pour into an 8 cup mold. Chill 8 hours. Serves 12.

Christmas Salad

1 (3 ounce) package lime
   gelatin
1 (15-1/2 ounce) can crushed
   pineapple
Juice from pineapple plus
   water to make 1 cup
1 (8 ounce) package cream
   cheese

1-1/2 cups miniature
   marshmallows
1 (8 ounce) carton Cool Whip
2 (3 ounce) packages raspberry
   gelatin
2 cups boiling water
1 (12 ounce) package frozen
   raspberries, thawed

Dissolve lime gelatin in a large mixing bowl with 1 cup of boiling pineapple juice and water. Add cream cheese and beat on slow speed of mixer. Add marshmallows and pineapple and fold in Cool Whip. Pour into a Pam sprayed 9 x 13 glass dish and refrigerate until set. In separate bowl, dissolve raspberry gelatin with the 2 cups boiling water. Add raspberries and pour over first layer of gelatin mixture. Refrigerate.

When slicing hard-cooked eggs, wet the knife before each cut to keep yolks from crumbling.

Shrimp Monterey Salad

1 pound cooked tiny shrimp
2 tablespoons grated
   Parmesan cheese
1/4 cup oil
3 tablespoons red wine vinegar
1 tablespoon lemon juice
2 teaspoons Dijon mustard

1/2 teaspoon black pepper
1/2 teaspoon salt
3 medium avocados, peeled
   and halved
1-1/2 cups grated Monterey
   Jack cheese

Combine shrimp and Parmesan cheese in a bowl with a lid. Mix together the oil, vinegar, lemon juice, mustard, pepper and salt. Pour dressing over shrimp and marinate 2 hours. Place 1 avocado half in each of 6 individual ramekins. Divide seafood evenly onto the avocados halves. Sprinkle with Monterey Jack cheese. Serve immediately.

Crunchy Chicken Salad

4-1/2 cups cooked, chopped
   chicken breasts
1 (8 ounce) can water chestnuts
1 cup celery
1 cup green grapes, sliced in
   half
1 (2.25 ounce) package sliced
   almonds

Dressing:
1 (3 ounce) package cream
   cheese, softened
1 cup mayonnaise
1 tablespoon lemon juice
1 tablespoon Grey Poupon
   Dijon mustard
1/2 teaspoon black pepper
1 teaspoon salt
Lettuce

In a large bowl, combine chicken, water chestnuts, celery, grapes and almonds. In a smaller bowl, combine cream cheese and mayonnaise and mix with a fork until the cream cheese is smooth. To the cream cheese and mayonnaise mixture, add the lemon juice, mustard, pepper and salt. Fold the dressing into the chicken mixture. Serve on a bed of lettuce. Refrigerate. Serves 8.

Almond Chicken Salad

3-1/2 cups cooked, chopped
   chicken breasts
1-1/2 cups chopped celery
1/2 apple, peeled, diced
1/2 (8 ounce) can crushed
   pineapple, well drained
1 cup toasted slivered almonds

1 cup red grapes, cut in half
1-1/2 teaspoons salt
1 teaspoon dry mustard
1/4 teaspoon pepper
3 tablespoons lemon juice
1/4 cup sour cream
1 cup mayonnaise

In a large mixing bowl, combine chicken, celery, apple, pineapple, almonds and grapes. Add salt, mustard, pepper, lemon juice, sour cream and mayonnaise and toss. Refrigerate. Serves 8.

Curry Chicken Salad

1 (8 ounce) package cream
   cheese, softened
1/2 cup mayonnaise
3 cups chopped, cooked
   chicken breasts
1 cup chopped walnuts

1/2 cup flaked coconut
1-1/2 teaspoons curry powder
1 teaspoon salt
1/2 teaspoon white pepper
Lettuce

In a medium bowl, mix cream cheese and mayonnaise together and blend well. Add remaining ingredients; stir together well. Serve on a lettuce leaf.

Add your tomatoes to the salad last as they tend to thin salad dressings.

Crunchy Tuna Salad

2 (7 ounce) cans white tuna in
    water, drained
1/4 cup chopped onion
1/2 cup chopped celery
1/4 cup chopped ripe olives

1 (2 ounce) jar chopped
    pimentos
2/3 cup mayonnaise
1 tablespoon wine vinegar
1 (3 ounce) can chow mein
    noodles

In a mixing bowl, combine all ingredients except noodles and refrigerate. Just before serving, toss with noodles. Serves 4 to 6.

Molded Tuna Salad

3 envelopes plain gelatin
1/2 cup cold water
1 can cream of chicken soup
2 cans tuna, rinsed
1 cup mayonnaise

1 cup chopped celery
3 boiled eggs, chopped
1-1/2 teaspoons Worcestershire
1/2 cup chopped stuffed olives

Mix gelatin and water and let dissolve. In a medium saucepan, heat the soup and stir in gelatin; mix well and set aside. In a mixing bowl, combine tuna, mayonnaise, celery, eggs, Worcestershire and olives; mix. Add soup mixture and pour into Pam greased mold or a greased 8 x 12 inch glass dish.

Avocado Salad

1 (3 ounce) package lime
    gelatin
1-1/2 cups boiling water
1 (8 ounce) package cream
    cheese
1/4 cup chopped bell pepper

1/2 cup chopped celery
2 tablespoons minced onion
1/4 teaspoon salt
1/2 cup mayonnaise
2 teaspoons lemon juice
1 avocado, well mashed

In a mixing bowl, dissolve gelatin in boiling water. Add cream cheese and stir with a whisk until cheese is mostly dissolved. Add remaining ingredients and mix. Pour into a 6 to 8 cup mold. Refrigerate.

Soups

Tortilla Soup

1 onion, chopped
1 (4 ounce) can chopped green
    chilies
2 cloves garlic, minced
2 tablespoons oil
1 cup tomatoes, peeled and
    chopped
1 bell pepper, chopped
1 (14 ounce) can beef broth
1 (14 ounce) can clear chicken
    broth
1-1/2 cups water

1-1/2 cups tomato juice
1 teaspoon cumin
2 teaspoons chili powder
1 teaspoon coriander
1 teaspoon salt
1 teaspoon freshly ground
    pepper
2 teaspoons Worcestershire
6 corn tortillas, cut into 1/2
    inch strips
1 cup grated Cheddar cheese

Saute onion, chilies and garlic in oil until soft. Add tomatoes, bell pepper, beef and chicken broth, water, tomato juice, cumin, chili powder, coriander, salt, pepper and Worcestershire. Bring soup to a boil; lower heat and simmer, covered for 1 hour. Just before ready to serve, add tortillas and cheese and simmer for 10 minutes. Serves 6.

Quick Vegetable Soup

1 pound ground beef
1 (16 ounce) can mixed
    vegetables
1 (1 ounce) envelope onion
    soup mix

1 (46 ounce) can cocktail
    vegetable juice
3 cups water
1/3 cup macaroni
1 tablespoon instant beef
    bouillon

In a roaster, brown the ground beef, stirring to crumble; drain off any fat. Add all remaining ingredients and bring to a boil. Lower heat and simmer for about 1 hour. Serves 8.

Use crispy Chinese noodles, canned onion rings, or potato sticks for an unusual crunch to the top of soup or stews.

Cream of Zucchini Soup

1 small onion, finely chopped
2 tablespoons margarine
3-1/2 cups unpeeled zucchini,
   diced in a food processor
1 (14-1/2 ounce) can chicken
   broth

1 teaspoon seasoned salt
1 teaspoon dill weed
1/2 teaspoon white pepper
1 (8 ounce) carton sour cream

In a saucepan, saute onion in margarine until onion is just lightly cooked. Using the food processor, chop the zucchini with the metal blade. Add zucchini, broth, seasoned salt, dill weed and pepper to the onion. Cover and simmer 10 to 15 minutes. Stir in sour cream; mix well and bring to boiling point. Remove from heat and serve. Serves 4.

Mex-Tex Soup

1 onion, chopped
1 green pepper, chopped
1 (16 ounce) can Mexican Style
   Stewed Tomatoes
2 (10-1/2 ounce) cans chicken
   broth
1 can water

1 teaspoon dried oregano
1 teaspoon chili powder
1 teaspoon ground cumin
1/2 teaspoon pepper
1 bay leaf
1 cup diced, cooked chicken
   breasts

Combine all ingredients in a Dutch oven. Bring to a boil; reduce heat, cover and simmer for 1 hour. Remove bay leaf before serving.

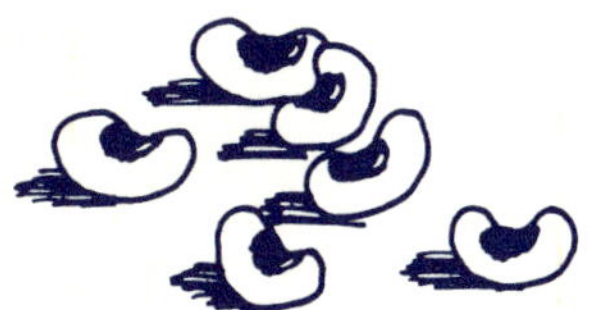

To garnish vegetable soup, top with grated cheese. To garnish consomme, garnish with lemon slices.

Chili Chicken Stew

4 cups cooked, cut up chicken
   pieces
1 chopped onion
1 chopped bell pepper
2 cloves garlic, minced
1 (14-1/2 ounce) can stewed
   tomatoes, undrained
1 (15 ounce) can pinto beans,
   undrained
1 can water

2/3 cup picante sauce
1 teaspoon chili powder
1 teaspoon ground cumin
1/2 teaspoon salt
1 tablespoon instant chicken
   bouillon
Shredded Cheddar cheese
   (optional)
Sliced green onions
   (optional)

In a large Dutch oven, combine all ingredients, except Cheddar cheese and green onions. Bring to a boil and then simmer for 30 minutes. Top individual servings with cheese and green onions. Serves 6.

Baked Onion Soup

6 yellow onions, thinly sliced
1/4 teaspoon sugar
1 garlic clove, minced
1 stick margarine
2 cans beef broth
1 can water

1/2 cup dry sherry
6 slices French bread, sliced 1
   inch thick, well toasted
3/4 cup finely grated Gruyere
   cheese*

In a saucepan saute onions, sugar and garlic in the margarine until lightly browned. Add the broth, water and sherry. Bring to a boil; then simmer until the onions are tender. Ladle soup into 6 individual oven proof crock bowls. Place one slice of the toasted bread slices in each bowl of soup. Top each serving with 1/6th of the cheese. Bake in 375 degree oven until the cheese has melted. Serve hot. *If you cannot find the Gruyere cheese, you can substitute Swiss cheese.

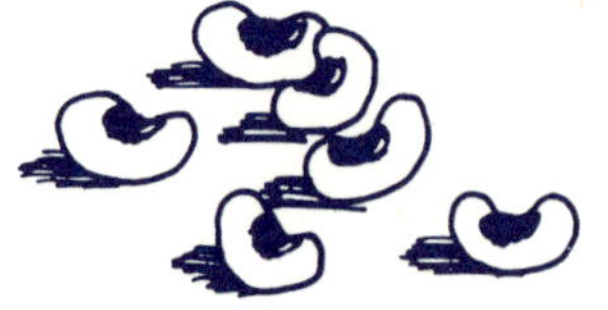

Instant mashed potatoes can be added as a thickener for stews, soups and casseroles for a richer taste.

Potato Cheese Soup

4 large potatoes, cubed
2 carrots, sliced
Water
2 stalks celery, sliced
1 onion, finely grated
1/2 stick margarine
3 tablespoons instant chicken
    bouillon
1 teaspoon seasoned salt

1/4 teaspoon ground thyme
1/2 teaspoon crushed rosemary
1/4 teaspoon garlic powder
1/2 teaspoon white pepper
2 cups half and half or Milnot
1-1/2 cups grated Cheddar
    cheese
3 slices bacon, cooked and
    chopped

In a large saucepan, cook potatoes and carrots with just enough water to cover vegetables. When cooked, mash with potato masher or with the mixer (do not drain water off). Carrots will remain chunky. In a small saucepan, saute celery and onion in margarine. Add to mashed potatoes in the large saucepan. Add remaining ingredients except bacon. Bring to a boil, lower heat and simmer for 10 minutes. Serve with bacon pieces sprinkled over individual bowls of soup. Serves 6 to 8.

Broccoli Soup

1 (10 ounce) package frozen
    chopped broccoli
1 (10 ounce) can chicken broth
1/2 onion, very finely chopped
1 stalk celery, very finely
    chopped
3 tablespoons margarine
2 tablespoons flour
2-1/2 cups milk

1 teaspoon salt
1/2 teaspoon sweet basil
1/2 teaspoon white pepper
1/2 teaspoon garlic powder
1/4 teaspoon cumin
1/8 teaspoon Tabasco
1 cup grated American or
    Cheddar cheese

Cook broccoli according to directions; drain. (You could microwave broccoli for 9 minutes, stirring once). Puree the broccoli with the chicken broth in food processor or blender. In a large saucepan, saute the onion and celery in the margarine. Add flour and mix. Add the milk; cook, stirring constantly until mixture has thickened just a little. Add salt, basil, white pepper, garlic powder, cumin, Tabasco and the pureed broccoli. Cover and simmer for about 15 minutes. Add cheese and heat just until cheese is melted. Soup will not be smooth; it is delightfully chunky and rich.

Vegetables

Baked Squash Ole

4 to 5 cups cooked squash, drained
1 teaspoon salt
1/2 teaspoon pepper
1 onion, chopped
1 (4 ounce) can chopped green chilies, drained
3/4 cup grated Monterey Jack cheese
1 (10-3/4 ounce) can cream of chicken soup
1 cup sour cream
1 stick margarine, melted
1 package herb dressing mix

Place cooked squash in a mixing bowl and season with salt and pepper; add onion, green chilies, cheese, soup and sour cream. Blend well. Mix margarine and herb dressing mix. Place 1/2 of the dressing mix in a 9 x 13 inch greased baking dish; pour squash mixture on top. Sprinkle with remaining dressing mix. Bake at 375 degrees for 30 minutes. Serves 10.

Posh Squash

2 pounds yellow squash, sliced
1 onion, chopped
1/2 pound Velveeta cheese, cubed
2 eggs, beaten
1 tablespoon sugar
1 (4 ounce) jar chopped pimento
1 teaspoon salt
1 teaspoon white pepper
6 tablespoons margarine, melted
Topping:
2 cups cracker crumbs
1/2 stick margarine, melted
1 (6 ounce) can fried onion rings

Boil squash and onion together until tender. Drain and mash with a potato masher. Add cheese; cook, stirring constantly over low heat until cheese is melted. Add remaining ingredients, except topping and blend well. Pour into a 9 x 13 inch greased casserole dish. Mix crumbs and margarine and sprinkle over casserole. Bake at 350 degrees for 45 minutes. Add fried onion rings to top and bake an additional 5 minutes.

It takes 2 tablespoons flour to make 1 tablespoon cornstarch.

Texanna Zucchini Bake

4 cups zucchini squash,
  cooked, drained and
  mashed
1/2 bell pepper, finely chopped
1 stick margarine, melted
1 (10 ounce) can cream of
  celery soup
1/2 teaspoon salt
1/2 teaspoon white pepper
1 onion, finely chopped
1 (2 ounce) jar chopped
  pimento
1 cup sour cream
3 cups herb-seasoned stuffing
1/2 cup grated Parmesan cheese
Paprika

In a mixing bowl, combine the squash, bell pepper, margarine, soup, salt, pepper, onion, pimentos, sour cream and the stuffing. Pour the mixture into a 2-1/2 quart buttered casserole dish. Top with grated cheese and sprinkle with paprika. Bake at 350 degrees for 25 minutes or until bubbly. Serves 8 to 10.

Southwest Zucchini

5 cups sliced zucchini squash
1/4 cup water
1 bell pepper, chopped
1 onion, chopped
1 stalk celery, chopped
4 tablespoons margarine
3/4 teaspoon seasoned salt
1/2 teaspoon pepper
2 eggs
1 (4 ounce) can chopped green
  chilies
1 cup mayonnaise
1-1/2 cups grated Cheddar
  cheese
1-1/2 cups cracker crumbs

Cook zucchini for 5 to 10 minutes in water just until partially tender. In a skillet, saute pepper, onion and celery in margarine; add salt and pepper. Combine eggs, green chilies, mayonnaise and cheese. Drain zucchini well. Combine all vegetables and egg-mayonnaise mixture and pour into a 3 quart casserole. Sprinkle crumbs over casserole and bake at 350 degrees for 30 minutes.

Melt 1/2 stick margarine in skillet; add 10 to 12 crushed club crackers and saute until golden brown. Sprinkle over buttered pasta or green vegetables for a simply spectacular treat.

Creamy Squash

6 to 8 medium yellow squash
Water
1 (8 ounce) package cream
   cheese, softened

2 tablespoons margarine
3/4 teaspoon salt
3/4 teaspoon pepper
1/2 teaspoon sugar

Cut squash in little pieces and place in a large saucepan. Cover with water and boil 10 to 15 minutes or until tender. Drain liquid off squash and add cream cheese that has been cut in chunks, margarine, salt, pepper and sugar. Cook over low heat, stirring until cream cheese has melted. Serve hot. Serves 8.

Summer Squash

2 pounds yellow squash, cut
   up
1 (3 ounce) package cream
   cheese, cubed
4 green onions, chopped
1/2 stick margarine, melted

1 teaspoon salt
1/2 teaspoon pepper
1-1/2 cups bread crumbs
1/4 stick margarine, melted
1/4 cup grated Parmesan cheese

Cook squash in a large saucepan until tender. Drain and mash. Stir in cream cheese while squash is still hot so cream cheese will melt. Add onion, 1/2 stick melted margarine, salt and pepper. Pour into a buttered 1-1/2 quart casserole dish. Mix together the bread crumbs, 1/4 stick margarine and Parmesan cheese. Sprinkle on top of squash. Bake at 350 degrees for 25 minutes. Serves 8.

Do not salt water that is to be used for boiling corn, it toughens the corn.

Jalapeño Spinach Bake

2 (10 ounce) packages frozen
    chopped spinach
1/2 stick margarine
1/2 cup chopped onion
3 tablespoons flour
2/3 cup milk or Milnot
1/2 teaspoon salt

1/2 teaspoon pepper
1/2 teaspoon celery salt
1/2 teaspoon garlic powder
Several dashes of Tabasco
8 ounces Jalapeño Velveeta
    cheese
1 cup cracker crumbs

Cook spinach according to package directions. Or the spinach can be microwaved in the box at 5 minutes for each box at high. Just be sure to punch a few holes in tops of boxes. Melt margarine in a large saucepan and add onion and flour; cook a minute or two (don't turn burner so high that the margarine will burn). Add the milk, salt, pepper, celery salt, garlic powder and Tabasco. Cook on low until mixture is thickened. Add Jalapeño cheese that has been cut in chunks and keep on low heat, stirring until cheese has melted. Add spinach to saucepan and stir until blended. Pour into a greased 3 quart baking dish. Top with cracker crumbs. Bake at 350 degrees for 25 minutes. Serves 8 to 10.

Cheesy Spinach

2 (10 ounce) packages frozen
    chopped spinach
1 (8 ounce) package cream
    cheese, softened

3 tablespoons margarine,
    melted
2 tablespoons grated
    Parmesan cheese
3/4 cups cracker crumbs

Cook spinach according to package instructions or microwave the boxes of spinach on high for 5 minutes each. Punch a few holes in each box before microwaving. In a mixing bowl, combine cream cheese and margarine. Beat at medium speed until smooth. Add Parmesan cheese and spinach; mix thoroughly. Spoon into a buttered 2 quart casserole and cover with cracker crumbs. Bake uncovered at 350 degrees for 25 minutes. Serves 6 to 8.

White onions are milder that yellow onions.

No-Crust Spinach Quiche

1 bunch green onions,
    chopped (tops too)
2 small zucchini, grated
2 teaspoons dill weed
1/2 stick margarine
2 (10 ounce) packages chopped
    spinach, thawed and
    squeezed very dry
1 pound Ricotta cheese

1 teaspoon instant chicken
    bouillon
4 eggs, lightly beaten
Several dashes Tabasco
3/4 cup grated Mozzarella
    cheese
3/4 cup grated Cheddar cheese
1 teaspoon salt
1/2 teaspoon pepper

In a large skillet saute the first 3 ingredients in the margarine until soft. Add the remaining ingredients to mixture in skillet and blend well. Spoon into a greased 9 inch springform pan and bake at 350 degrees for one hour or until set. Serves 8 to 10.

Texas Fried Okra

3/4 cup yellow cornmeal
3/4 cup flour
1-1/2 teaspoons salt
1/4 teaspoon pepper

1 pound (about 4 cups) fresh
    okra
1 tablespoon buttermilk or
    milk
1/3 cup oil

In a plastic bag, combine cornmeal, flour, salt and pepper. Cut okra into 1/2 inch slices and pour buttermilk over okra and toss. Place okra in plastic bag and shake. In a skillet, heat oil and add okra. Fry on moderate heat, turning frequently, until crispy and brown. Drain on paper towels. Serve immediately.

Add a teaspoon of sugar to fresh green beans for an extra dash of flavor.

Green Bean Ole

2 cans French cut green beans
1 cup sour cream
8 ounces Jalapeño Velveeta
   cheese, cut in chunks
1/2 onion, minced

1/2 teaspoon pepper
2 cups crushed Rice Crispies*
3 tablespoons margarine,
   melted

Drain green beans well. Butter a 2-1/2 quart baking dish. In a large saucepan, melt the sour cream and Jalapeño Velveeta cheese, stirring constantly. Add onion, pepper and green beans, mix. Pour into the buttered baking dish. Combine crushed Rice Crispies and margarine and sprinkle over green bean mixture and bake at 350 degrees for 30 minutes. Serves 8 to 10. (Corn flakes will work well too.)

Party Green Beans

1/2 stick margarine
1 onion, chopped
2 (2 ounce) cans sliced button
   mushrooms, drained
1 (2 ounce) jar chopped
   pimientos
1/4 cup flour
1 cup half and half or Milnot
   evaporated milk
1 (8 ounce) jar Mild Mexican
   Cheese Whiz

1/4 teaspoon Tabasco
1 tablespoon soy sauce
1/2 teaspoon salt
1/2 teaspoon pepper
1 (6 ounce) can sliced water
   chestnuts, drained
3 (16 ounce) cans whole green
   beans, drained
1 (2-1/4 ounce) package
   slivered almonds

In a large skillet, melt margarine and saute the onion. On medium heat, add mushrooms, pimientos and flour and stir well. Add half and half or milk and the Cheese Whiz and stir until cheese has melted and the mixture is thick. Add remaining ingredients except the almonds; mix well. Pour into a greased 9 x 13 inch baking dish and top with almonds. Bake at 350 degrees for 20 to 25 minutes or until bubbly. Serves 12.

When steaming vegetables like zucchini, broccoli and fresh asparagus, add a tablespoon of lemon juice for a light aroma and flavor.

Green Bean Supreme

2 tablespoons margarine
2 tablespoons flour
1 teaspoon salt
1/2 teaspoon pepper
1/2 onion, chopped
1 teaspoon sugar
1 cup sour cream
2 cans green beans, drained
12 ounces Swiss cheese, grated
2-1/2 cups cracker crumbs

Melt margarine in a saucepan and stir in flour, salt, pepper, onion and sugar. Add sour cream and mix well. In a large mixing bowl, mix together the sour cream mixture, green beans and Swiss cheese. Pour into a 2-1/2 quart buttered baking dish and sprinkle cracker crumbs over the top. Bake at 350 degrees about 25 to 30 minutes. Serves 8 to 10.

Baked Mexican Green Beans

1 onion, chopped
1/2 stick margarine
2 tablespoons flour
2 cups heavy cream or Milnot
1/2 package Taco Seasoning
    Mix
1 teaspoon instant chicken
    flavor bouillon
1 (4 ounce) can chopped green
    chilies, drained
2 (16 ounce) cans green beans
1 cup grated Monterey Jack
    cheese
1 cup grated sharp Cheddar
    cheese

In a large skillet, saute the onion in the margarine until soft. Add the flour and stir to a thick paste. Add the cream, Taco seasoning, chicken bouillon and green chilies. On medium heat, stir until sauce begins to thicken. Place the beans in a 3 quart baking dish and pour sauce over them. Bake at 350 degrees for 20 minutes. Remove from oven and sprinkle both cheeses over green beans and cook 10 more minutes. Serves 8 to 10.

Creamy Cauliflower

1 (16 ounce) package frozen
    cauliflower
1/2 cup sour cream
3 tablespoons margarine
8 ounces Mild Mexican
    Velveeta

Cook cauliflower according to directions on package. In a medium saucepan, combine sour cream, margarine and cut up Velveeta. Melt on low heat. Pour over cauliflower. Serve immediately.

Parmesan Peas

2 (10 ounce) packages frozen
  green peas
3 tablespoons margarine,
  melted
1/4 cup grated Parmesan cheese
2 tablespoons minced onion

1/8 teaspoon dried lemon peel
1 tablespoon lemon juice
1/2 teaspoon salt
1/8 teaspoon dried tarragon
  leaves

Cook peas as directed on package and drain. Toss with remaining ingredients. Serve hot. Serves 6 to 8.

Sunshine Green Peas

2 cans LeSueur sweet peas
1 cup sour cream
8 ounces Swiss cheese, grated
1/2 onion, minced

1/2 teaspoon pepper
2 cups crushed corn flakes
3 tablespoons margarine

Drain peas well. In a large saucepan, melt the sour cream and Swiss cheese, stirring constantly. Add onion, pepper and peas; mix. Pour into a buttered baking dish. Combine the crushed Corn Flakes and margarine and sprinkle over peas. Bake at 350 degrees for 30 minutes. Serves 8 to 10.

*To substitute 1/3 cup chopped raw onion,
use 2 tablespoons instant minced onion.*

Sesame Peas

1 (10 ounce) package frozen
   green peas
1/2 stick margarine

2 tablespoons sesame seed
1 teaspoon sugar
1/4 teaspoon salt

Cook peas as directed on package and drain. In a medium saucepan, cook remaining ingredients over medium heat, stirring constantly, until golden brown. Pour over peas. Serve hot. Serves 4.

Classic Cauliflower

2 (10 ounce) packages frozen
   cauliflower
4 slices bacon
1 can cream of chicken soup
1 cup cracker crumbs, divided

1/2 cup sour cream
1 (2 ounce) jar chopped
   pimentos
1/2 cup grated Cheddar cheese

Cook cauliflower according to package directions — just until tender. Drain and place in a medium sized, greased baking dish. Fry bacon crisp and crumble, set aside. In a medium saucepan, mix soup, 1/2 cup crumbs, sour cream, pimentos and cheese. Heat just until all ingredients are well mixed. Pour over cauliflower and top with remaining crumbs. Bake at 350 degrees for 20 to 25 minutes. Sprinkle crumbled bacon over casserole before serving.

Add a pinch of soda to green vegetables while cooking to retain color.

Crunchy Pecan Broccoli

1 (16 ounce) package frozen
broccoli (not chopped)
1 (10 ounce) package frozen
cauliflower
1/8 cup water
1 package dried onion soup
mix
3/4 stick margarine, melted
and divided

1/2 cup water
2/3 cup chopped pecans
1 (5 ounce) can sliced water
chestnuts, drained
3/4 cup grated Cheddar cheese
2-1/2 cups Rice Krispies,
crushed

Place broccoli and cauliflower in a casserole dish with a lid. Add 1/8 cup water. Microwave for 6 minutes, stirring twice. (Or cook lightly by conventional method). In a larger mixing bowl, combine soup mix, 1/2 of the melted margarine, 1/2 cup water, pecans, water chestnuts and cheese; mix. Add the cooked, drained broccoli and cauliflower to the soup-pecan mixture. Toss and place in a greased 2-1/2 quart or a 9 x 13 inch greased baking dish. Add remaining margarine to the crushed Rice Krispies; mix. Top casserole with Rice Krispies. Bake, uncovered in the 350 degree oven for 25 minutes.

Baked Broccoli and Cauliflower

1 (10 ounce) package frozen
broccoli
1 (10 ounce) package frozen
cauliflower
1 egg
2/3 cup mayonnaise

1 can cream of chicken soup,
undiluted
1 cup grated Swiss cheese
1 onion, chopped
1 cup bread crumbs
1/4 stick margarine
Paprika

Cook broccoli and cauliflower as directed on packages. Drain well and place in large mixing bowl. In a saucepan, combine egg, mayonnaise and soup and heat. Pour over vegetables; add cheese and onion and mix well. Pour into a 9 x 13 buttered baking dish. Combine bread crumbs and margarine and sprinkle over broccoli and cauliflower mixture. Sprinkle paprika over top. Bake at 350 degrees for 30 to 35 minutes. Serves 8 to 10.

Impossible Broccoli Pie

1 (16 ounce) package frozen
   chopped broccoli, thawed
12 ounces grated Cheddar
   cheese, divided
2/3 cup chopped onion

3 eggs
3/4 cup buttermilk biscuit mix
1-1/2 cups milk
3/4 teaspoon salt
3/4 teaspoon pepper

Cut large chunks of the broccoli into smaller pieces. In a large mixing bowl, combine broccoli, 2/3 of the cheese and onion; mix. Pour into a greased 10 inch deep-dish pie plate. In the same mixing bowl, mix eggs and biscuit mix; beat for a couple of minutes. Add milk, salt and pepper and mix until fairly smooth. Pour over broccoli and cheese mixture. Bake at 375 degrees for 35 to 40 minutes or until knife inserted in center comes out clean. Top with remaining cheese and bake just until cheese is melted. Let stand 5 minute before serving. Serves 6 to 8.

Asparagus Caesar

2 (14-1/2 ounce) cans
   asparagus, drained
1/2 cup margarine, melted

3 tablespoons lemon juice
2/3 cup grated Parmesan cheese
1 cup croutons

Rinse asparagus and drain again. Arrange in a greased baking dish and drizzle with margarine and lemon juice. Sprinkle with cheese. Bake at 400 degrees for 15 minutes or until bubbly. Take out of oven and sprinkle with croutons. Bake 5 minutes more. Serves 6.

Never add salt to dry beans that you are cooking until they are already tender or they will remain hard.

Asparagus Cheese Bake

2 (15 ounce) cans cut asparagus
 spears, reserve liquid
3 hard-cooked eggs, chopped
1/2 cup chopped pecans
1 can cream of asparagus soup,
 mixed with the asparagus
 liquid

1/2 stick margarine
1/2 teaspoon black pepper
2 cups cracker crumbs
2 cups Monterey Jack cheese,
 grated

Arrange the drained asparagus spears in a buttered 2 quart casserole dish. Top with chopped eggs and pecans. Heat asparagus soup, liquid from the can of asparagus, margarine and pepper. Pour over asparagus, eggs and pecans. Combine cracker crumbs and cheese. Sprinkle over casserole. Bake at 350 degrees for 25 minutes. Serves 8.

Sesame Asparagus

1/3 cup mayonnaise
1/2 cup sour cream
1/2 teaspoon seasoned pepper
2 tablespoons sesame seeds,
 lightly toasted

2 (10 ounce) cans cut spears
 asparagus
1 cup crushed cracker crumbs

In a small bowl, stir together mayonnaise, sour cream, seasoned pepper and sesame seeds. Mix well. Drain asparagus and place in a greased 6 by 10 inch baking dish. Spoon mayonnaise mixture over asparagus and spread over top. Sprinkle cracker crumbs over top. Bake at 350 degrees for 25 to 30 minutes, until cracker crumbs are lightly browned. Serves 6.

Zucchini Bake

1/3 stick margarine
6 cups grated zucchini squash
 (unpeeled)
1/2 teaspoon pepper

1/2 teaspoon garlic powder
1/2 cup sour cream
1 cup crushed cheese cracker
 crumbs

Melt margarine in a large skillet; add zucchini, pepper and garlic powder; heat. After zucchini begins to cook, turn burner to medium heat and cook 8 minutes, stirring several times. Turn burner off; add sour cream and mix. Pour into a 2 quart greased casserole. Top with cracker crumbs. Bake uncovered at 350 degrees for 25 minutes or until crumbs are lightly browned.

Green Chili Hominy

2 (17 ounce) cans hominy, drained
1 (8 ounce) can chopped green chilies
1/4 cup finely grated onion

1-1/2 cups grated Cheddar cheese
1 (8 ounce) carton sour cream
3/4 teaspoon seasoned salt
1/4 teaspoon pepper

Mix all ingredients together and pour into a medium size greased casserole dish. Bake at 350 degrees for 30 to 35 minutes.

Best Little Bean in Texas

3 cups dried pinto beans
Water
1/2 pound diced salt pork*
4 jalapeño peppers, chopped
1 onion, chopped

2 tablespoons chili powder
2 teaspoons garlic powder
1 teaspoon oregano
2 teaspoons salt

Wash beans, cover with water and let soak overnight. Add the remaining ingredients, except salt; bring to a boil. Reduce heat and let simmer in a covered pot about 4 hours. Add hot water if needed. Keep beans covered until serving time. Add salt before serving. Serves 8. *A ham hock could be used in place of the salt pork.

A few drops of lemon juice in water will whiten boiled potatoes.

Fiesta Corn

1 (16 ounce) can cream style
   corn
1 (16 ounce) can whole kernel
   corn, drained
1 bell pepper, chopped
1 small onion, chopped
1 (4 ounce) can chopped green
   chilies
1/4 stick margarine, melted
2 eggs
1 tablespoon sugar

1/2 teaspoon salt
1/2 teaspoon pepper
1/2 cup buttery cracker crumbs
2 tablespoons grated
   Parmesan cheese
1 cup grated Cheddar cheese
Topping:
3/4 buttery cracker crumbs
2 tablespoons grated
   Parmesan cheese
Paprika to garnish

Grease a 9 x 13 inch baking dish. In a large mixing bowl, mix together all ingredients except topping and pour into the baking dish. Top with cracker crumbs and Parmesan and garnish with the paprika. Bake in a 350 degree oven for 45 minutes. Serves 8 to 10.

Shoe Peg Corn

1 stick margarine
1 (8 ounce) package cream
   cheese
3 (16 ounce) cans shoe peg
   corn, drained

1 (4 ounce) can chopped green
   chilies
1/2 teaspoon seasoned salt
1/2 teaspoon white pepper
1-1/2 cups crushed cracker
   crumbs

Melt margarine in a large saucepan and stir in cream cheese. Mix until well blended. Add corn, chilies, salt and pepper. Mix; pour into a medium baking dish that has been greased. Sprinkle cracker crumbs over casserole. Bake at 350 degrees for 25 minutes. Serves 8 to 10.

Chicken broth adds a flavorful and low calorie seasoning on vegetables in place of butter.

Creamy Macaroni and Cheese

1 (12 ounce) package macaroni
2/3 stick margarine
1/4 cup flour
2 cups milk

1 pound Velveeta cheese,
 cubed
1 teaspoon salt
1/2 teaspoon white pepper

Cook macaroni according to package directions and drain. Melt margarine in a saucepan and stir in flour until well blended. Add milk and heat until it begins to thicken, stirring constantly. Add cheese and stir until cheese melts. Add cheese sauce to macaroni and mix well. Pour into a buttered 2-1/2 quart baking dish and bake at 350 degrees for 30 minutes or until bubbly. Serves 10.

Three Cheese Spaghetti

1/2 (12 ounce) package
 spaghetti, broken up
4 tablespoons margarine
1 tablespoon flour
1 cup milk
1 cup grated Gouda cheese
1 cup grated Cheddar cheese

1 (2-1/2 ounce) can sliced
 mushrooms, drained
1 (4 ounce) can chopped green
 chilies, drained
1 tablespoon dried parsley
 flakes
1/4 teaspoon salt
1/2 cup grated Parmesan cheese

Cook spaghetti as directed on package. Melt margarine in a heavy saucepan and add flour, stirring until smooth. Gradually add milk, stirring constantly until thick and bubbly. Stir in Gouda and Cheddar cheese, mushrooms, chilies, parsley and salt. Stir until cheeses are melted. Pour cheese sauce into spaghetti; mix. Pour into a 2 quart greased baking dish. Sprinkle Parmesan cheese over top. Cook at 375 degrees for 15 to 20 minutes or until bubbly. Serves 8.

To make bread crumbs, cut 6 slices of bread into 1 inch cubes. Microwave in a 3 quart casserole for 4 minutes, stirring after 2 minutes. Make crust in food processor.

Oven Fried Potatoes

3 medium potatoes
1/4 cup vegetable oil
1 tablespoon grated Parmesan
   cheese

1/2 teaspoon salt
1/4 teaspoon garlic powder
1/4 teaspoon paprika
1/4 teaspoon pepper

Preheat oven to 375 degrees. Scrub potatoes. Leaving skins on potatoes, cut into 1/8 inch wedges. Place wedges slightly overlapping in a single layer in a 9 x 13 x 2 inch baking dish. Combine oil, cheese, salt, garlic powder, paprika and pepper, stirring well. Brush potatoes with half of oil mixture. Bake uncovered for 45 minutes, basting occasionally with remaining oil mixture. Serves 4 to 6.

Parmesan Potatoes

1-1/4 stick margarine
1/2 cup flour
2/3 cup grated Parmesan cheese
1-1/2 teaspoons salt

1/2 teaspoon pepper
1/8 teaspoon cayenne
5 medium to large potatoes,
   peeled

Melt the margarine in a 9 x 13 inch baking dish and set aside. Mix together flour, cheese, salt, pepper and cayenne and place in a bag. Quarter the potatoes lengthwise and then cut each quarter in half again lengthwise. While potatoes are still wet, place them in the bag with seasoning. Shake and toss until the potatoes are thoroughly covered. Place the potato strips in the baking dish with the margarine. Arrange the potatoes in a single layer and bake at 375 degrees for 1 hour, turning once after 30 minutes. Serves 8.

Easy Cheese Potatoes

1 onion, chopped
1 cup chopped celery
3 tablespoons margarine
1 can cream of celery soup

1 (3 ounce) package cream
   cheese
1 (12 ounce) package frozen
   hash browns, thawed
1 cup grated Cheddar cheese

Saute onions and celery in margarine until barely tender. Stir in undiluted soup and cream cheese. Heat and stir until creamy. In a 2 quart casserole, make 2 layers each of potatoes, soup mixture and cheese; ending with cheese. Cover and bake at 375 degrees for about 40 minutes.

Oven Potatoes

1/2 cup water
2 teaspoons instant chicken
    bouillon
3/4 cup heavy cream or Milnot

1-1/2 cups grated Cheddar
    cheese
3 large potatoes, peeled
Salt
Pepper

Heat water and add chicken bouillon; stir. Stir in cream and grated cheese. Slice potatoes and place in a 2-1/2 quart buttered baking dish. Pour bouillon and cream mixture over the potatoes. Sprinkle salt and pepper over top. Cover and bake at 350 degrees for 30 minutes; then uncover and bake for another 30 minutes. Serves 6 to 8.

Super Mashed Potatoes

8 medium potatoes, peeled,
    cooked, drained and
    mashed
1 (8 ounce) package cream
    cheese

1 (8 ounce) carton sour cream
3/4 stick margarine
1 teaspoon salt
1/2 teaspoon pepper
Paprika

Place potatoes in large mixing bowl and whip until fluffy. Add cream cheese, sour cream, margarine, salt and pepper. Whip until cream cheese, sour cream and margarine are melted. Pour into a 3 quart baking dish and garnish with paprika. Cook at 350 degrees for about 20 to 25 minutes.

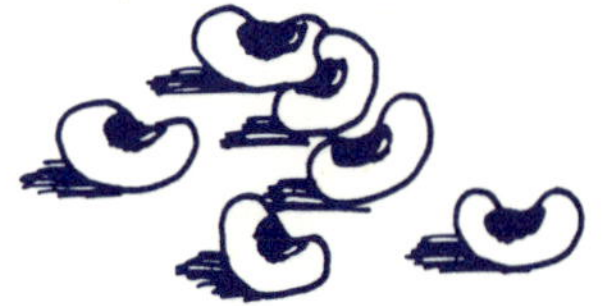

If you add a little milk to the water in which cauliflower is cooking, the cauliflower will retain its white color.

Jalapeño Cheese Potatoes

4 potatoes, cooked, peeled and
  sliced
4 green onions, tops too,
  chopped
1 bell pepper, chopped
2 tablespoons margarine
1/2 stick margarine
1 tablespoon flour

1 teaspoon salt
1/2 teaspoon white pepper
1/2 teaspoon garlic powder
1 cup milk
1 (2 ounce) jar chopped
  pimentos
8 ounces Jalapeño Velveeta
  cheese

Place sliced potatoes in a 9 x 13 inch buttered baking dish. In a medium saucepan, saute onion and bell pepper in the 2 tablespoons margarine. Add the 1/2 stick margarine and melt; add flour, salt, white pepper and garlic powder. Stir well and add milk, stirring until mixture thickens. Add pimentos and cheese, cut in chunks. Simmer until cheese melts. Pour the sauce over potatoes and bake at 350 degrees for 45 minutes. Serves 8.

Cheddar Potato Casserole

1 (2 pound) bag frozen hash
  brown potatoes, thawed
1 onion, finely chopped
1 stick margarine, melted
1 cup sour cream

1 can cream of chicken soup
2 cups Cheddar cheese, grated
1-1/2 cups corn flakes, crushed
1/2 stick margarine, melted

In a large mixing bowl, combine hash browns, onion, margarine, sour cream, soup and cheese; mix well. Pour into a greased 9 x 13 inch baking dish. Combine corn flakes and melted margarine and sprinkle on casserole. Bake at 350 degrees for 45 minutes.

Shrimply Delicious Potatoes

Baked potatoes

1 recipe Curried Shrimp Dip
  on page 16

Top baked potatoes with Curried Shrimp Dip. Add a tossed salad and French toast and you have a meal.

Chili Cheese Grits

1-1/2 cups uncooked grits
6 cups water
3 eggs
1 stick margarine
1 pound shredded Longhorn
    cheese

3 teaspoons seasoned salt
1 teaspoon salt
1 teaspoon Tabasco
1 (4 ounce) can chopped green
    chilies
Paprika

Bring water to a boil and add grits slowly and cook until done. Beat eggs and add with remaining ingredients to hot grits. Stir until cheese and margarine melt and pour into a greased 9 x 13 inch baking pan. Bake at 275 degrees for 1 hour and 20 minutes (longer if center is not set). This can be prepared ahead of time and baked right before serving.

Cheesy Rice Bake

2-3/4 cups water
1 package dry chicken-noodle
    soup mix
1 cup uncooked rice
1 can cream of chicken soup
1 cup grated Cheddar cheese

3/4 cup evaporated milk or
    Milnot
1 (2 ounce) jar chopped
    pimentos
1 cup grated Cheddar cheese

In a medium to large saucepan, combine water, soup mix and rice. Bring to a boil and simmer 15 minutes, stirring twice while simmering. Add remaining ingredients, except for the last cup of cheese. Blend well. Pour into a greased 3 quart baking dish. Bake at 350 degrees for 25 minutes. Remove from oven and sprinkle on the remaining cup of cheese. Return to oven for 5 minutes. Serves 8 to 10.

Sour Cream Rice

1 cup raw rice
1 (4 ounce) can chopped green
    chilies
1/4 stick margarine, melted
1-1/4 cups sour cream

1/2 teaspoon salt
1/2 teaspoon white pepper
1/2 pound grated sharp
    Cheddar cheese*

In a large saucepan, cook rice as directed on package. When rice is cooked, add all remaining ingredients and mix thoroughly. If your rice cooked fairly dry, you might add 1/3 cup water to the mixture so it won't be too dry. Pour into a greased 2 quart casserole and bake covered, 35 to 40 minutes at 350 degrees. *This is good made with Mozzarella cheese instead of Cheddar cheese.

Quick Dinner Rice

1 cup white rice, uncooked
1-1/4 cups water
1 stick margarine, melted
1 teaspoon salt
1/2 teaspoon white pepper
3/4 teaspoon garlic powder

1/4 cup dried parsley
1 onion, chopped
1 egg, beaten
8 ounces Jalapeño Velveeta
    cheese
1 cup milk

Butter a 2 quart baking dish. Mix all ingredients, except the Velveeta cheese and milk, into the buttered baking dish. Cut the cheese in chunks and place cheese and milk in a saucepan on low heat, stirring until cheese has melted. Mix in with the rice mixture and stir well. Cook, covered at 350 degrees for 55 minutes. Serves 8.

Texas Rice

1 cup chopped green onion
1/2 stick margarine
3 cups cooked white rice
1 cup sour cream
1/2 cup small curd cottage
    cheese
1 teaspoon salt

3/4 teaspoon pepper
1 (4 ounce) can chopped green
    chilies
1 cup grated sharp cheese or
    Monterey Jack cheese
Paprika

Saute onion in margarine. Remove from heat and combine with remaining ingredients except paprika. Toss lightly to mix and pour into a greased casserole dish. Bake at 350 degrees for 30 to 35 minutes. Garnish with paprika. Serves 8.

To keep spaghetti or noodles from boiling over, add 1 teaspoon oil to the boiling water.

Main
Dishes

Adobe Chicken

2 cups cooked white rice
2 cups cooked brown rice
1 (16 ounce) can stewed
    tomatoes, drained
1 onion, chopped
3 cups cooked chicken, cut
    into 1/2 inch cubes
1/2 teaspoon salt
1/2 teaspoon pepper
2 (4 ounce) cans chopped
    green chilies
2 cups sour cream
3 cups shredded Monterey
    Jack cheese
1 (2-1/4 ounce) can sliced ripe
    olives, drained

In a large bowl, combine white and brown rice, tomatoes, onion, cubed chicken, salt, pepper and green chilies. Spoon half the mixture into a greased 3 quart casserole. Cover with 1 cup of sour cream, 1-1/2 cups cheese and all of the olives. Repeat layering with remaining chicken mixture, sour cream and cheese. Bake uncovered at 350 degrees for 45 minutes. Let stand 10 minutes before serving. Serves 8.

Green Rice Chicken

1/2 cup chopped green bell
    pepper
1/2 cup chopped celery
3/4 cup chopped green onions,
    tops too
1 stick margarine
1-1/2 cups uncooked rice
1 (8 ounce) carton sour cream
2-1/2 cups cooked chicken
    breasts, deboned and cut
    up
2-2/3 cups hot chicken broth
1 (4 ounce) can chopped green
    chilies
1 teaspoon salt
1/4 teaspoon pepper

Saute bell pepper, celery and onions in margarine. Spray a large, covered casserole dish with Pam or butter lightly. Combine all ingredients and bake covered at 350 degrees for 35 minutes. Uncover and cook another 10 minutes.

When marinating meats, place the meat and the marinade in a heavy-duty plastic bag, press out air bubbles and seal. The marinade stays close to the meat and you don't dirty a pan to wash.

Sesame Chicken

1/2 cup flour
1/2 teaspoon chili powder
1/4 teaspoon paprika
1/2 teaspoon onion salt
1/2 teaspoon celery salt
1 teaspoon lemon pepper
1 teaspoon garlic powder
8 skinned chicken breasts
1 stick margarine, melted
1 cup sesame seeds, lightly
  toasted

Thoroughly mix flour, chili powder, paprika, onion and celery salt, lemon pepper and garlic powder. Roll chicken breasts in flour mixture; keep rolling chicken until all flour mixture is used up. Dip floured chicken in margarine and then roll in sesame seeds. Place chicken breasts into a greased 9 x 13 baking dish. Pour any extra margarine over chicken. Bake at 325 degrees for one hour, turning after 30 minutes.

Savory Chicken

1 (2-1/2 ounce) jar dried beef
  slices
8 chicken breasts, boned and
  skinned
Pepper
1 can cream of chicken soup
1 cup sour cream
1 teaspoon summer savory
3 slices bacon
Hot cooked rice

Line a greased 9 x 13 inch baking dish with dried beef slices. Sprinkle chicken breasts with pepper and place over the dried beef. Mix soup, sour cream and savory; heat slightly; pour this mixture over top of chicken. Cover and bake 1 hour at 325 degrees. While chicken is cooking, fry bacon and chop. 5 minutes before chicken is done, take out of oven and sprinkle chopped bacon over chicken and return to oven for 5 minutes, uncovered. Serve over hot rice.

To slice or grind chicken in a food processor, freeze slightly before processing.

Fiesta Chicken

1 stick margarine, divided
1-3/4 cups finely crushed
    Cheddar cheese crackers
2 tablespoons Taco Seasoning
    Mix
6 to 8 chicken breasts, boned,
    skinned and flattened
5 green onions, tops too,
    chopped

1 (4 ounce) can chopped green
    chilies
2 cups heavy cream or Milnot
1 teaspoon instant chicken
    bouillon
2 cups grated Monterey Jack
    cheese

Melt margarine in a 9 x 13 inch baking dish and set aside. Combine cracker crumbs and taco mix. Dredge chicken in this mixture — pat this on so you get plenty of crumbs to stick on chicken. Place chicken in baking dish with margarine. In a medium size saucepan, take out a couple tablespoons of the melted margarine and place in saucepan. To the melted margarine in saucepan, add chopped onions and saute. Then add the green chilies, heavy cream or Milnot, instant chicken bouillon and the Monterey Jack cheese; mix well. Pour this mixture over chicken breasts. Bake uncovered at 350 degrees for 50 to 55 minutes. Serves 6 to 8.

Chicken Mexicana

6 or 8 chicken breasts, boned
    and skinned
Pepper
1/2 stick margarine
1 onion, chopped
4 green onions, tops too,
    chopped
1 bell pepper chopped
1 (4 ounce) can chopped green
    chilies

1 (15 ounce) can stewed
    tomatoes
1/2 cup catsup
1 teaspoon instant chicken
    bouillon
1 tablespoon cumin
1 tablespoon basil
1 tablespoon cilantro
Garnish:
Sour cream (optional)

Season chicken with pepper. In a large heavy skillet, brown the chicken on both sides in the margarine. Do not turn heat up so high that the margarine burns. Transfer chicken to a buttered 9 x 13 inch shallow baking dish. In the same skillet saute the onions and bell pepper until soft, adding more margarine if necessary. Add the remaining ingredients except garnish and simmer 5 minutes. Pour sauce over the chicken and bake at 350 degrees, covered for 35 minutes. Top with sour cream.

Old Fashioned Chicken Spaghetti

8 to 10 ounces spaghetti
1 bell pepper, chopped
1 onion, chopped
1 cup chopped celery
1 stick margarine
1 can tomato soup
1 can Rotel diced tomatoes and
    green chilies
1 small can chopped
    mushrooms
1/2 teaspoon salt

1/2 teaspoon pepper
1/2 teaspoon garlic powder
3 teaspoons chicken bouillon
1/2 cup water
4 to 5 cups chopped chicken or
    turkey*
6 ounces Velveeta cheese,
    chopped
6 ounces Cheddar cheese,
    chopped

Cook spaghetti according to package instructions. Drain. In a medium sauce-pan, saute bell pepper, onion and celery in margarine. Add soup, Rotel tomatoes, mushrooms, salt, pepper, garlic powder, bouillon and water; mix. In a large mixing bowl, mix spaghetti, soup and tomato mixture, chicken and cheese. Place in 2 greased 2-quart casseroles. Freeze one and bake the other (covered) for 40 to 50 minutes at 325 degrees. To cook the frozen casserole, thaw first. *This is a good recipe to use leftover turkey.

Apricot Chicken

1 cup apricot preserves
1 (8 ounce) bottle Catalina
    dressing

1 package onion soup mix
8 chicken breasts

In a bowl, mix apricot preserves, dressing and soup mix. Place chicken breasts in a large, buttered baking dish and pour apricot mixture over chicken. Bake uncovered at 325 degrees for 1 hour and 20 minutes.

The flavors of garlic, pepper and cloves get stronger when frozen. The flavors of salt, onion or sage get milder when frozen.

Spiced Glazed Chicken

1/4 stick margarine
6 chicken breasts
Salt and pepper

1-1/2 cups apricot preserves
3/4 cup Catalina dressing
Cooked rice

In a skillet, melt margarine and brown breasts. Sprinkle with salt and pepper. Place chicken in buttered baking dish. Mix preserves and dressing together in a saucepan and heat. Pour over chicken and bake uncovered at 350 degrees for 1 hour, basting chicken every 15 minutes. Serve over cooked rice.

Orange Glazed Cornish Hens

1 (5 ounce) package brown
   and wild rice mix
1 onion, chopped
2 stalks celery, chopped
1 tablespoon margarine,
   melted
1/8 teaspoon poultry seasoning
4 (1-1/4 pound) Cornish hens
Salt

Melted margarine
Orange Glaze:
1/4 cup sugar
1/2 cup orange juice
1/2 teaspoon grated orange
   rind
1 tablespoon margarine
1-1/2 teaspoons lemon juice

Prepare rice according to package directions; set aside. Saute onion and celery in the 1 tablespoon margarine. Combine vegetables, rice and poultry seasoning. Remove giblets from hens. Rinse hens with cold water and pat dry. Sprinkle cavities with salt. Stuff hens lightly with rice mixture. Close cavities and secure with wooded picks. Place hens breast side up and in a shallow baking pan; brush with melted margarine. Bake at 375 degrees for 1-1/2 hours, basting occasionally with margarine. Spoon orange glaze over hens and bake 5 minutes longer. For the Orange glaze, combine sugar, orange juice and orange rind in a small saucepan. Bring to a boil. Remove from heat; add margarine and lemon juice. Stir until margarine melts. Serves 8.

For grilling chicken, use the margarine, apricot preserves and the Catalina dressing in the Spiced Glazed Chicken recipe on this page for basting grilled chicken. Use basting several times during grilling.

Southern Fried Chicken

1 chicken, cut up
Salt and pepper
2 eggs, beaten
2 tablespoons cream
Flour
Oil or shortening

Gravy:
3 tablespoons flour
1/2 teaspoon salt
1/2 teaspoon pepper
1-1/2 cups whole milk

Salt and pepper each piece of chicken. Add cream to the beaten eggs and dip chicken into egg mixture and roll in the flour, coating chicken well. Heat about 1/4 inch oil or shortening in a heavy skillet; brown chicken on both sides. Lower heat and cook until tender, about 25 minutes. For gravy, remove chicken from the skillet and add the 3 tablespoons flour, salt and pepper. Stir and turn burner to high heat. Add milk and cook, stirring until gravy thickens. Serve hot.

Chicken Enchiladas

2 cups cooked, shredded
   chicken
1 (4 ounce) can chopped green
   chilies
1 (7 ounce) can green chili salsa
1 onion, very finely chopped
6 chicken bouillon cubes

1/2 teaspoon salt
2-1/2 cups heavy cream
Oil
12 corn tortillas
2 cups grated Monterey Jack
   cheese
1 (8 ounce) carton sour cream

Combine chicken, green chilies, green chili salsa and onion. Place bouillon cubes, salt and cream in a saucepan and heat until bouillon is dissolved — but do not boil. Heat oil in skillet and dip each tortilla into oil for about 5 seconds, just to soften. Drain on paper towels. Then dip each tortilla into saucepan with cream, coating each side. Fill each tortilla with chicken mixture. Roll and place seam side down in a baking dish. Pour remaining cream over enchiladas and sprinkle with cheese. Bake uncovered at 350 degrees for 30 to 35 minutes. When ready to serve, top with dollops of sour cream.

If soup or sauce is too salty, add slices of raw potato and cook 10 or 15 minutes. Remove potato slices that have absorbed the excess salt.

Chicken Doritos

6 large boneless chicken
   breasts
1 (9-1/2 ounce) bag Doritos
1 onion, finely chopped
1 cup chopped celery

1 can chicken soup
2 (10 ounce) cans Rotel
   tomatoes and green chilies
1 pound Velveeta cheese

In a large saucepan, boil the chicken breast in water about 25 to 30 minutes, until done. Let cool and cut into small bite-size pieces. Spray a 9 x 13 inch baking dish with Pam and place 1/2 of the bag of Doritos in dish. Crush a little with your hand. In a large saucepan, combine onion, celery, chicken soup, tomatoes and green chilies and Velveeta. On medium heat, stir until cheese is melted. Add chicken pieces and pour over Doritos. Crush remaining Doritos in a zip-top bag with rolling pin. Sprinkle over chicken-cheese mixture. Bake at 350 degrees about 30 minutes or until bubbly around edges.

Chicken Parmesan

3 whole chicken breasts, split,
   boned and skinned
Pepper
1 egg, slightly beaten
1 tablespoon water
1-1/2 cups cracker crumbs
Oil
2 (8 ounce) cans tomato sauce

1/4 teaspoon sweet basil flakes
1/4 teaspoon garlic powder
1/4 teaspoon savory
2 tablespoons margarine
1/3 cup water
1/2 cup grated Parmesan cheese
6 slices Mozzarella cheese

Place chicken on cutting board, using a meat mallet, flatten to 1/4 inch thickness. Pepper the 6 pieces of chicken. Dip breasts into egg and 1 table-spoon water. Then dip breasts in the cracker crumbs, patting to get plenty of the crumbs. In a large skillet, brown chicken in oil; drain on paper towels. Place chicken in a greased 9 x 13 inch baking dish. Pour oil out of skillet. Combine, in the skillet, the tomato sauce, basil, garlic, savory, margarine and water. Simmer 2 or 3 minutes. Pour mixture over chicken breasts and sprinkle with Parmesan cheese. Cover and bake at 350 degrees for 30 minutes. Uncover and place 1 slice cheese over each chicken breast. Bake an additional 5 minutes. Serves 6.

Texas Chicken-Fried Steak

2 pounds round steak,
   tenderized
1-1/4 cups flour
1 teaspoon salt
Seasoned pepper
2 eggs, slightly beaten
1/2 cup milk
Oil

Cream gravy:
6 to 8 tablespoons pan grease
   or bacon drippings
6 tablespoons flour
3 cups milk
1/2 teaspoon salt
1/4 teaspoon pepper

Trim steak and cut into 6 to 8 pieces. Combine flour, salt and pepper. Dredge all steak pieces in flour mixture until lightly coated. Combine eggs and milk. Dip steak into egg mixture and dredge again in flour, getting plenty of flour mashed into steak. Heat 1/2 inch of oil in a heavy skillet and fry steak pieces on medium to low heat about 25 to 30 minutes or until golden brown. To make gravy, remove steaks to a warm oven, retaining drippings. Add flour. Cook and stir until flour only begins to brown. Add milk and stir until thickened. Season with salt and pepper and serve over steaks or mashed potatoes.

Texas Chili

3 tablespoons oil, divided
1 pound lean ground beef
1 pound lean boneless beef,
   cut into 1/2 inch cubes
2 onions, chopped
4 cloves garlic, minced
1/4 cup tomato paste
4 fresh or canned jalapeño
   peppers, stemmed, seeded
   and minced
5 tablespoons chili powder
1 teaspoon salt

1 teaspoon oregano
1 tablespoon cumin
1 teaspoon black pepper
2 (14-1/2 ounce) cans tomatoes,
   undrained
1 (10-1/2 ounce) can condensed
   beef broth
2 cups water
2 (4 ounce) cans chopped
   green chilies, undrained
1 (15 ounce) can pinto beans

Heat 1 tablespoon of oil in a 5 quart kettle; crumble in ground beef and add cubed beef. Cook, stirring occasionally until meat is lightly browned. Transfer meat to a bowl. Heat remaining 2 tablespoons oil in kettle and add onion and garlic. Cook 3 minutes and stir in tomato paste, jalapeño peppers, chili powder, salt, oregano, cumin and black pepper. Coarsely chop tomatoes and add to kettle. Add meat, beef broth, water and green chilies. Bring to a boil and reduce heat. Simmer partially covered for 2 to 2-1/2 hours or until meat is very tender and chili has thickened. Stir in beans and continue simmering uncovered for another 20 minutes. Spoon into individual bowls and serve with lots of crackers.

Impossible Taco Pie

1 pound ground beef
1/2 cup chopped onion
1 envelope taco seasoning mix
1 (4 ounce) can chopped green
    chilies
1-1/4 cups milk
3/4 cup biscuit mix

3 eggs
Topping:
1-1/2 cups grated Cheddar
    cheese
Sour Cream
Picante Sauce

In a large skillet, brown ground beef and onion; drain off any fat. Stir in seasoning mix and green chilies. Spread in a greased 10 inch quiche dish or a 10 inch pie plate. Beat milk, biscuit mix and eggs together until smooth (about 1 minute with an electric mixer). Pour into pie plate with meat and bake 25 minutes at 400 degrees. Take out of oven and sprinkle with cheese. Return to oven and cook 5 to 8 minutes longer. Cool 5 minutes before slicing. Serve with a dab of sour cream and Picante Sauce. Serves 8.

Taco Pie

1 (8 ounce) can crescent rolls*
2 cups crushed Doritos or
    Fritos
1 pound lean ground beef

1 (8 ounce) jar of hot taco sauce
1 cup sour cream
1-1/2 cups grated Cheddar
    cheese

Place the crescent rolls into a 9 inch pie pan, pulling and pinching the dough to form a pie crust. Sprinkle half the chips on the pie crust. Brown meat and drain. Add taco sauce; mix. Spoon meat mixture over chips. Spoon sour cream on top. Sprinkle on the grated cheese and top with remaining chips. Bake at 350 degrees for 20 minutes. *A regular pie crust could also be used.

Allow roasted meat or fowl to stand at room temperature for about 15 minutes before slicing.

Marvelous Meat Loaf

1 pound ground turkey
1 pound ground beef
2 eggs
1 envelope onion soup mix
1/4 cup catsup
1/4 cup minced bell pepper
1/2 cup sour cream
1/2 teaspoon garlic powder

1/2 teaspoon pepper
2 teaspoons Worcestershire
1 cup crushed crackers
Topping:
1-1/4 cups catsup
1 cup brown sugar
3 tablespoons Dijon mustard
Several shakes Tabasco

In a large mixing bowl, combine all meat loaf ingredients and mix well. Place meat mixture on a greased 9 x 13 inch baking pan and shape it like a loaf. Make it about the size of a loaf pan only with rounded corners. While meat is cooking, mix the topping in a medium saucepan. Heat. Serve the topping for meat loaf separately in a gravy boat. Serves 8.

Tortilla Bake

1 pound lean ground beef
1 onion, chopped
1 (14 ounce) can stewed
   tomatoes
1 (10 ounce) can hot enchilada
   sauce
1/2 pound Velveeta, cut in
   chunks
2 teaspoons ground cumin
1/2 teaspoon salt

1/2 teaspoon pepper
2 cups crushed Tortilla chips
6 flour tortillas
1 (3 ounce) package cream
   cheese, softened
1 (4 ounce) can chopped green
   chilies
1 cup grated Monterey Jack
   cheese

In a skillet, brown beef and onion. Drain off fat. Stir in tomatoes, enchilada sauce, Velveeta, cumin, salt and pepper. On low heat, cook until cheese is melted. Place crushed Tortilla chips in a greased 9 x 13 inch baking pan. Pour two-thirds of the beef mixture over Tortilla chips. Warm the 6 flour tortillas until they are soft. Spread tortillas with the cream cheese; top with green chilies. Fold tortillas in half and arrange folded tortillas in a line over the meat mixture. (They will overlap a little.) Pour remaining meat down center. Cover and bake at 350 degrees for 20 minutes. Uncover and sprinkle cheese on top. Return to oven for 5 minutes. Serves 6.

Smothered Steak

1-1/2 pounds beef round or
   sirloin steak, about 3/4
   inch thick
Salt and pepper
1/3 cup flour
3 tablespoons oil

3 medium onions, sliced
1 (10 ounce) can beef broth
1 tablespoon lemon juice
1 teaspoon garlic powder
1/4 teaspoon dried thyme
1/2 teaspoon summer savory

Cut meat into serving sized pieces. Salt and pepper steak pieces and dip in flour. Pound the flour into the steak with a meat tenderizer. Brown steak in the oil. Top with onion slices and stir in remaining ingredients. Bring to a boil; reduce heat to a simmer. Cover and cook slowly for one hour. Check steak while cooking; you may need to add a little water. Serves 6 to 8.

Texas Enchiladas

Oil
1-1/2 pounds lean ground beef
1 onion, finely minced
1 clove garlic, minced
1/2 teaspoon salt
2 cups water
2 tablespoons chili powder
3 tablespoons oil
2 tablespoons flour

1 (16 ounce) can tomato sauce
1/2 teaspoon salt
1/2 teaspoon pepper
1/2 teaspoon cumin
12 corn tortillas
Oil
1 pound Cheddar cheese,
   grated

Place a very little bit of oil in skillet and brown beef, onion and garlic; add salt. Combine water and chili powder and set aside. In a saucepan, heat 3 tablespoons oil and add flour, stirring until browned. Slowly add chili powder mixture, stirring until thickened. Add tomato sauce, salt, pepper and cumin and simmer 5 minutes. Soften tortillas by dipping in a little hot oil; drain. Place about 2 tablespoons of meat mixture in each tortilla, top with cheese and roll. Place seam side down in a baking dish, cover with sauce and any remaining meat mixture and cheese. Bake at 350 degrees for 35 minutes or until hot and bubbly.

When boiling shrimp, add a stick of celery to the water. It eliminates the strong odor of the shrimp.

Bar B Q Brisket

4 to 6 pound beef brisket	Bar B Q sauce:
2 tablespoons Worcestershire	1 cup ketchup
Seasoned salt	1/3 cup Worcestershire
Garlic powder	3/4 cup brown sugar
Black pepper	1 tablespoon lemon juice
1/2 cup water	

Place brisket in shallow baking pan. Pour Worcestershire over the brisket. Sprinkle with seasoned salt, garlic powder and pepper; add water to the pan. Cover with foil. Bake at 425 degrees for 30 minutes. Lower oven to 250 degrees and cook for about 4 hours. While brisket is cooking, mix all sauce ingredients together in a saucepan. When brisket is done, add pan dripping to sauce. Chill brisket; slice in thin slices and pour sauce over slices and return to oven until brisket is warm.

Cheeseburger Pie

1 pound lean ground beef	1 (9 inch) deep dish pie crust
1/2 onion, chopped	Cheese topping:
1 tablespoon oil	1 beaten egg
1/2 teaspoon oregano	1/2 teaspoon dry mustard
1/2 teaspoon black pepper	1/2 teaspoon Worcestershire
1/2 teaspoon salt	1/4 cup milk
1/4 cup chili sauce	2 cups grated American cheese
1 (8 ounce) can tomato sauce	

In a skillet, brown beef and onion in oil; drain any fat off. Add remaining ingredients except cheese topping and simmer about 5 minutes. Pour into pie crust. For topping, mix all ingredients together and pour over meat mixture. Cook at 375 degrees for about 30 minutes or until center of cheese layer is firm. Serves 6.

To remove odor of fish from hands, rub them with lemon juice or vinegar before washing.

Chili Relleno Casserole

1 pound lean ground beef
1 bell pepper, chopped
1 onion, chopped
1 (4 ounce) can chopped green
    chilies
1 teaspoon oregano
1 teaspoon dried cilantro
    leaves
1/2 teaspoon garlic powder
1/2 teaspoon salt

1/2 teaspoon pepper
1 (7 ounce) can whole green
    chilies*
1-1/2 cups grated Monterey
    Jack cheese
1-1/2 cups grated sharp
    Cheddar cheese
3 large eggs
1 tablespoon flour
1 cup half and half or Milnot

In a skillet, brown meat with the bell pepper, onion, the 4 ounce can of green chilies, oregano, cilantro, garlic powder, salt and pepper. Seed whole chili peppers and spread on the bottom of a greased 9 x 13 inch baking dish. Cover with meat mixture and sprinkle with cheeses. Combine eggs and flour, beat with fork until fluffy. Add half and half; mix and pour over top of meat in casserole. Bake in a 350 degree oven for 30 to 35 minutes or until it is lightly browned. *You could use the chopped green chilies instead of the whole green chilies.

Peach Glazed Pork Roast

1-1/2 cups peach-flavored
    wine cooler
1 teaspoon dried rosemary
    leaves
1 teaspoon seasoned salt
1 teaspoon dry mustard
1 teaspoon finely shredded
    lemon rind

2 cloves garlic, crushed
1/2 teaspoon pepper
4 to 5 pound boneless
    tenderloin pork roast
1/2 cup peach preserves
1 tablespoon cornstarch
1 tablespoon water

Mix together the wine cooler, rosemary, seasoned salt, mustard, lemon rind, garlic and pepper. Place roast in a shallow glass baking dish. Cover with wine cooler mixture. Place lid on baking dish or cover with foil and refrigerate, turning several times. Marinate at least 12 to 24 hours. When ready to cook, pour off about 1/2 cup of the marinade and cook, uncovered in a 325 degree oven for 2-1/2 hours. Spoon pan drippings over pork occasionally. Remove from oven; spoon peach preserves over roast and bake about an hour more. Remove roast and pour pan drippings in a saucepan. Mix cornstarch and water; add to pan drippings. Stirring well, heat to boiling and cook 1/2 minute. Serve this sauce with the roast. Let roast set at room temperature 10 to 15 minutes before slicing.

Barbecued Pork Chops

6 boned pork chops
Salt
Pepper
Paprika
2 tablespoons oil
1 onion, sliced in 6 slices

2/3 bottle chili sauce
2 tablespoons Worcestershire
2 tablespoons brown sugar
1/4 teaspoon Tabasco
1/4 cup water

Season the pork chops well with salt, pepper and paprika. In a skillet with the oil, brown pork chops well on both sides. Place pork chops in a medium size baking dish and place one slice of onion on top of each chop. Mix together the chili sauce, Worcestershire, brown sugar, Tabasco and water. Pour this sauce over the chops and onion. Cover and bake at 300 degrees for 35 to 40 minutes.

Ranch Pork Chops

6 to 8 pork chops
2 tablespoons oil
1 cup chili sauce
1 (10 ounce) can Rotel
    tomatoes and chilies
1/2 cup plum jelly

1/2 package Hidden Valley
    Ranch Dressing mix
6 green onions, tops too,
    chopped
2 garlic cloves, crushed

In a medium skillet, brown the pork chops in the oil. Then place the chops in a buttered 9 x 13 inch baking dish. In the same skillet, combine the chili sauce, Rotel tomatoes and chilies, jelly, dressing mix, green onions and crushed garlic. Let this mixture come to a boil and simmer 5 minutes. Pour over pork chops and bake, covered at 325 degrees for 1 hour.

When substituting dried herbs for fresh,
be sure to use only 1/3 as much.

Apricot Ribs

1 (17 ounce) can apricot halves
1/3 cup packed brown sugar
3 tablespoons vinegar
2 teaspoons soy sauce
1/2 teaspoon pepper
1/2 teaspoon salt
1 teaspoon garlic powder
1/2 teaspoon ground ginger
1 slab very lean pork ribs

Drain apricots, reserving 1/3 cup syrup. Puree apricots in the blender with the 1/3 cup reserved syrup. Pour into a small saucepan and add brown sugar, vinegar, soy sauce, pepper, salt, garlic powder and ginger. Stir and simmer over medium heat uncovered for 2 to 3 minutes. Place ribs in a 9 x 13 inch baking dish. Pour brown sugar-vinegar mixture over ribs and place in a 350 degree oven for 45 minutes. Lower heat to 300 degrees and cook another 3 hours.

Mexican Pork Chops

8 boned pork chops
2 tablespoons oil
1 onion, chopped
4 green onions, tops too, chopped
1 green pepper, chopped
2 tablespoons margarine
1 (4 ounce) can chopped green chilies, drained
1 (16 ounce) can stewed tomatoes
1/2 cup catsup
1 teaspoon instant beef bouillon
1 tablespoon cumin
1 tablespoon basil
1 teaspoon chili powder

In a large skillet, brown the pork chops on both sides in the oil. Place the browned chops in a buttered 9 x 13 inch shallow baking dish. In the same skillet saute the onions and green pepper in the margarine. Add remaining ingredients and simmer for 10 minutes. Pour over pork chops and bake, covered at 325 degrees for 1 hour.

Pork Chops and Apples

6 thick cut pork chops
Flour
Oil
3 baking apples

Dip pork chops in flour and coat well. In a skillet, brown pork chops in oil. Place in a 9 x 13 inch greased casserole. Add about 1/3 cup water to casserole. Cook, covered at 325 degrees for about 45 minutes. Peel, half and seed apples. Place 1/2 apple on top of each pork chop. Return to oven for 5 to 10 minutes. (Don't overcook apples.)

Blackened Redfish

Seasoning mix:
1 teaspoon onion powder
1 teaspoon cayenne pepper
1/2 teaspoon dried thyme
2-1/2 teaspoons salt
1 tablespoon paprika
1 teaspoon garlic powder

1/2 teaspoon white pepper
1-1/2 teaspoons black pepper
1/4 teaspoon dried oregano
8 to 10 serving size pieces of
   red fish fillets*
3 sticks of margarine or butter*

Thoroughly combine all seasonings. Dry fish fillets with scotch towels. Heat a heavy skillet to a very hot temperature. Dip fillets in margarine and then sprinkle seasoning mix on generously and evenly on both sides of the fillets, patting it in by hand. Place the fillets (2 at a time, depending on how large your skillet is) in the hot skillet and pour 1 teaspoon melted margarine on top of each fillet (be careful, margarine may flame up). Cook, uncovered over the high heat until underside looks charred, about 2 minutes (time will vary according to heat of the skillet). Turn the fish over and again pour 1 teaspoon margarine on top; cook another 2 minutes. Repeat with remaining fillets. Serve each fillet while piping hot. *If you only want to serve 2 to 4 fillets at a time, just melt 1 stick margarine and save the rest of the seasoning for another day.

Fried Fish

6 to 8 fillets
Salt
Pepper
1 cup buttermilk

2 cups very finely crushed
   cracker crumbs
1/3 cup flour
Oil

Dry fish with paper towels and season with salt and pepper on both sides. Mix the cracker crumbs with the flour. Dip the fish fillets into the buttermilk and then into the crumb mixture, coating heavily on both sides. In a large skillet, heat 1/2 to 1 inch of oil until it is very hot. Add the fish, a few pieces at a time. Fry for about 4 to 5 minutes on each side or until light brown. Serve at once.

All fish should be basted plentifully with butter or sauce during broiling.

Southwestern Baked Fish

6 orange roughy fillets*
1/2 cup sour cream
1 (3 ounce) package cream
    cheese
1 cup shredded white Cheddar
    cheese
1 tablespoon minced onion
1 tablespoon lemon juice

1/4 teaspoon garlic powder
1/2 teaspoon salt
1/4 teaspoon cayenne pepper
1/4 teaspoon minced cilantro
1 (4 ounce) can chopped green
    chilies
Paprika

Place fillets in a single layer in a greased baking dish. Blend sour cream and cream cheese until smooth. Add remaining ingredients except paprika and mix well. Spread over fish. Bake at 375 degrees for 15 to 20 minutes or until fish flakes easily. Garnish with paprika. *Red snapper or any white fish can be substituted for orange roughy.

Deep Fried Fish

Oil
2 pounds fish fillets or fish
    steaks
1 cup flour

1 teaspoon salt
1/4 teaspoon pepper
2 eggs, slightly beaten
1 cup dry bread crumbs

Heat oil (about 2 to 3 inches deep) in deep fryer or Dutch oven. If fillets are very large, cut into smaller serving size pieces. Mix flour, salt and pepper and coat fish with flour mixture. Dip into eggs and coat with bread crumbs. Fry in deep fryer until golden brown, about 5 minutes.

Broiled Trout Fillets

Fresh trout
Butter, melted
Salt

Pepper
Lemon juice

Cut the fish into serving pieces and marinate them in the warm melted butter seasoned with salt, pepper and lemon juice for about 30 minutes. Place them, dripping with butter, under a broiler and broil each side for 5 minutes. Baste with butter once again when fish is cooked. Serve immediately.

Orange Roughy Parmesan

4 serving size fillets of orange
   roughy, thawed
3 tablespoons lemon juice
2/3 cup grated Parmesan cheese
5 tablespoons margarine,
   melted

4 tablespoons mayonnaise
3 tablespoons finely chopped
   onion
1/4 teaspoon pepper
Several dashes Tabasco

In a foil lined 9 x 13 inch baking dish, place fillets in a single layer. Brush with lemon juice. Let stand 10 minutes. Broil 3 to 4 inches under preheated broiler for about 5 minutes or until slightly browned. Drain off any built up liquid. In a small bowl, combine cheese, margarine, mayonnaise, onion, pepper and Tabasco. Remove fillets from the oven after cooking time and spread cheese mixture over fillets. Broil another 2 to 3 minutes.

Gulf Coast Casserole

2 cans cream of chicken soup
1 tablespoon corn starch
2/3 cup mayonnaise
1 grated onion
1/4 cup milk
1/4 teaspoon nutmeg
1/4 teaspoon cayenne pepper
2 tablespoons Worcestershire
1/2 teaspoon salt
1/2 teaspoon pepper
2 tablespoons sherry

2-1/2 cups cooked shrimp,
   cleaned, deveined and
   drained
1 (7 ounce) can crab meat,
   drained
1 (5 ounce) can sliced water
   chestnuts, drained
1-1/2 cups chopped celery
3 tablespoons parsley, minced
Paprika
1 (2 ounce) package sliced
   almonds, toasted
Cooked rice

In a large mixing bowl, combine soup, corn starch, mayonnaise, onion and milk. Mix well. Stir in nutmeg, cayenne, Worcestershire, salt, pepper and sherry. Add well drained shrimp, crab meat, water chestnuts, celery and parsley. Mix well. Pour into a 3 quart buttered casserole. Top with paprika and almonds. Bake at 350 degrees for 45 minutes or until bubbly. Serve over rice. Serves 8.

Cakes
and
Cold
Desserts

White Chocolate Pound Cake

4 egg whites
6 ounces white chocolate*
1/2 cup water
1 cup shortening
1-3/4 cups sugar
2 eggs
1 teaspoon vanilla
2-1/2 cups flour
1 teaspoon baking soda
1/2 teaspoon baking powder

1 teaspoon salt
1 cup buttermilk
Glaze:
6 ounces white chocolate*
1 tablespoon margarine
1/4 cup hot water
1/4 cup sugar
Pinch of salt
1/4 cup light corn syrup
1 teaspoon vanilla

Beat egg whites until stiff but not dry; set aside. In top of double boiler, melt the chocolate with the water in top of double boiler. Set aside. In a mixing bowl, cream together the shortening and sugar until light and fluffy. Add eggs, one at a time, beating after each egg. Add white chocolate and vanilla; beat well. Add the flour, baking soda, baking powder and salt alternately with the buttermilk. Mix just until well blended. Fold beaten egg whites into the batter. Pour in a greased and floured bundt or tube pan and bake at 350 degrees for 50 to 55 minutes. Test with toothpick for doneness. Cool about 20 minutes before removing from pan. For the glaze: melt chocolate and margarine in top of double boiler. Add water, sugar, salt, corn syrup and vanilla. Heat, stirring until well blended. Gradually spoon over warm cake. Punch holes with toothpick so glaze will soak in cake. *Nestle's Premier White Baking Pieces or Bars can be used as the white chocolate.

White Chocolate Torte

Use recipe for White
    Chocolate Pound Cake
Frosting:
1 pint whipping cream
1/4 cup sugar

1 teaspoon vanilla
1 cup grated white chocolate
1 cup flaked coconut
1/2 cup chopped pecans

Instead of cooking in a tube pan, pour batter into 3 greased and floured 9 inch round cake pans. Bake at 350 degrees for 30 minutes. Test with toothpick for doneness. Cool for 15 minutes before removing from pan. Cool completely before frosting. To make frosting, whip cream with sugar and vanilla. Fold in grated white chocolate and coconut. Spread 1/3 on each layer and stack. Do not frost sides. Sprinkle pecans last on top layer. Refrigerate.

Chocolate Pound Cake

2 sticks margarine, softened
1/2 cup shortening
1 (3 ounce) package cream
    cheese, softened
3 cups sugar
2 teaspoons vanilla
5 large eggs
3/4 cup cocoa
3 cups flour

1 teaspoon baking powder
1/2 teaspoon salt
1 cup buttermilk
Icing:
1-1/2 cups powdered sugar
1-1/2 tablespoons cocoa
2 tablespoons milk
1/4 stick margarine, softened
1/4 teaspoon almond extract

In a large mixing bowl, cream together margarine, shortening, cream cheese and sugar. Beat at high speed for 5 minutes and add vanilla. Add eggs one at a time, beating well after adding each egg. In a separate bowl, mix together cocoa, flour, baking powder and salt. Add dry ingredients to the cream cheese mixture, alternately with buttermilk, ending with dry ingredients. Beat well for 3 minutes. Pour into greased and floured 10 inch tube pan and bake at 325 degrees for 1 hour and 10 to 15 minutes. Test with toothpick for doneness. Let cake rest in pan for 20 minutes; then turn onto cake plate; cool completely. For the icing, combine all ingredients and ice the top of cake, letting some icing run down the sides of the cake.

Chocolate Cherry Cake

1 milk chocolate cake mix
1 can cherry pie filling
3 eggs
Frosting:
5 tablespoons margarine

1-1/4 cups sugar
1/2 cup milk
1 (6 ounce) package chocolate
    chips

Combine cake mix, pie filling and eggs in mixing bowl. Mix by hand. Pour into a greased and floured 9 x 13 inch baking pan. Bake at 350 degrees for 35 to 40 minutes. Test cake for doneness with toothpick. When cake is done, combine margarine, sugar and milk in a medium saucepan. Bring to boiling point and boil 1 minute, stirring constantly. Add chocolate chips and stir until chips are melted. Pour over hot cake. Refrigerate.

Dust pan with equal parts of cocoa and flour to prepare pan for chocolate cake.

Milk Chocolate Pound Cake

2 sticks margarine, softened
1-1/2 cups sugar
4 eggs
4 (2.15 ounce) Milky Way bars
1 cup buttermilk
2-1/2 cups flour
1/4 teaspoon baking soda
5 ounces Hershey's chocolate syrup
2 teaspoons vanilla
1 cup chopped pecans

Frosting:
1-1/2 cups powdered sugar
6 tablespoons chocolate syrup

In a mixing bowl, cream margarine and sugar until light and fluffy. Add the eggs one at a time, beating well after each addition. In a small saucepan, melt the Milky Way bars on low heat and stir constantly. To the mixing bowl, add the melted Milky Way bars and buttermilk and mix well. Combine the flour and baking soda and stir into Milky Way mixture. Add chocolate syrup and vanilla and mix. Fold in the pecans. Pour into a greased and floured 10 inch tube pan and bake at 325 degrees for 1 hour. Test with toothpick for doneness. Cool completely. For the frosting: in a medium bowl, mix powdered sugar and 6 tablespoons chocolate syrup. Blend well and pour on top of cake. Let some of the frosting drip down the sides of the cake.

The Best Chocolate Cake

2 cups flour
2 cups sugar
2 sticks margarine
1 cup Coca Cola
3 tablespoons cocoa
1/2 cup buttermilk
2 eggs
1 teaspoon baking soda
1-1/2 teaspoons vanilla
2 cups miniature marshmallows

Frosting:
1 stick margarine, melted
2 cups powdered sugar
3 tablespoons Coca Cola
1 teaspoon vanilla
3 tablespoons cocoa
1 cup chopped pecans

In a mixing bowl, combine flour and sugar; mix. In a medium saucepan, heat the margarine, Coca Cola and cocoa just to the boiling point. Remove from heat and slowly pour into the flour mixture and mix well. Add buttermilk, eggs, baking soda and vanilla. Beat well. Stir in the marshmallows and pour batter into a greased and floured 9 x 13 inch baking pan. Bake at 350 degrees for 40 to 45 minutes. Test with toothpick for doneness. Let cake cool. Frosting: mix together the margarine, powdered sugar, Coca Cola, vanilla and cocoa and stir until it is completely smooth; add the pecans and frost cake.

To keep cheesecake from cracking while baking, put a pan of water on bottom rack of oven.

Chocolate Pudding Cake

1 milk chocolate cake mix
1-1/4 cups milk
1/3 cup oil
3 eggs
1 can sweetened condensed
    milk

3/4 of the milk can of
    chocolate syrup
1 (8 ounce) Cool Whip
1/3 cup chopped pecans

In a mixing bowl, combine cake mix, milk, oil and eggs. Beat well. Pour into a 9 x 13 inch greased and floured pan. Bake at 350 degrees for 35 to 40 minutes. Test with toothpick for doneness. In a small bowl, mix the sweetened condensed milk and the chocolate syrup. Pour over warm cake and let soak into cake. Chill several hours. Top cake with Cool Whip and sprinkle on pecans. Keep refrigerated.

Coconut Creme Cake

2-1/8 cups flour
1-1/3 cups sugar
4-1/4 teaspoons baking powder
1 teaspoon salt
1-1/2 sticks margarine,
    softened
1/2 cup milk
2 teaspoons vanilla
1 cup Coco Lopez Cream of
    Coconut Milk

6 egg whites, unbeaten
Syrup:
1 (15 ounce) can Coco Lopez
    Cream of Coconut Milk
1 can Eagle Brand milk
Topping:
1 (8 ounce) carton of Cool
    Whip
1 small can coconut

In a mixing bowl, mix together flour, sugar, baking powder, salt and margarine. Add milk and vanilla; beat for 2 minutes. Add 1 cup Cream of Coconut Milk and unbeaten egg whites. Beat for 3 to 4 minutes at medium to high speed. Pour into a greased and floured 9 x 13 inch baking pan. Bake at 350 degrees for 25 minutes; then lower oven temperature to 325 degrees and cook another 10 minutes or until cake tester comes out clean. Cool for 15 to 20 minutes. In a small mixing bowl, mix the can of Cream of Coconut Milk and the can of Eagle Brand milk. Perforate with ice pick the full depth of cake about every 1/2 inch and slowly pour mixture of Coconut milk and Eagle brand over cake evenly. Allow to cool at room temperature and top with Cool Whip; then sprinkle coconut on top. Keep refrigerated.

Before melting chocolate for a recipe, grease pot in which it is to be melted.

Poppy Seed Cake

3 cups sugar
1-1/4 cups shortening
6 eggs
3 cups flour
1/4 teaspoon soda
1/2 teaspoon salt
1 cup buttermilk
3 tablespoons poppy seeds

2 teaspoons almond extract
2 teaspoons vanilla
2 teaspoons butter flavoring
Glaze:
1-1/2 cups powdered sugar
1/3 cup lemon juice
1 teaspoon vanilla
1 teaspoon almond extract

In a large mixing bowl, cream sugar and shortening until mixture is light and fluffy. Add eggs, one at a time, blending mixture well. Sift together flour, soda and salt. Alternately add dry ingredients and buttermilk to the sugar mixture. Add poppy seeds and flavorings and blend well. Pour into a greased and floured bundt pan. Cook at 325 degrees for 1 hour and 15 to 20 minutes. Test with toothpick for doneness. For the glaze, combine all ingredients and mix well. Pour over top of cooled cake and let some of the glaze run down the sides of the cake.

Tropic Cake

2 cups flour
1-1/2 cups sugar
1/2 brown sugar
2 teaspoons baking soda
1/3 cup oil
2 eggs
1 (15 ounce) can crushed
    pineapple, undrained
1 teaspoon vanilla

Frosting:
1 box powdered sugar
1 (8 ounce) package cream
    cheese, softened
6 tablespoons margarine,
    softened
1/2 teaspoon orange extract
1 teaspoon vanilla
1 cup shredded coconut
1 cup chopped pecans

In a medium bowl combine the flour, sugars and soda. In a large mixing bowl, blend together the oil, eggs, pineapple and vanilla. Fold in the flour mixture and beat well. Bake in a 9 x 13 inch buttered and floured baking pan at 350 degrees for 35 minutes. Test with toothpick for doneness. For the frosting: Blend together powdered sugar, cream cheese, margarine and flavorings; beat until smooth. Fold in coconut and pecans. Ice cake while still hot. When cool, refrigerate.

The safest size egg to use in a recipe is a large egg.

Best Apple Cake

1-1/4 cups oil
2 eggs
2 cups sugar
2 cups flour
1 teaspoon salt
1 teaspoon nutmeg
1-1/4 teaspoons cinnamon
1 teaspoon soda
3 cooking apples, peeled and
  grated

1 cup chopped pecans
1 teaspoon vanilla
1/3 cup brandy
Glaze:
2 tablespoons margarine,
  melted
2 tablespoons milk
1-1/2 cups powdered sugar
1 teaspoon vanilla

In a large mixing bowl, combine oil, eggs and sugar and beat well. Add flour, salt, nutmeg, cinnamon and soda and mix well. Stirring by hand, add apples, pecans, vanilla and brandy and mix thoroughly. The batter will be very stiff, almost like a cookie dough. Pour into a greased and floured 9 x 13 inch baking dish and spread batter evenly. Bake in a 350 degree oven for 45 minutes. Test with toothpick for doneness. For the glaze, in a small bowl, combine all glaze ingredients and stir until smooth. Spread over hot cake.

Mystery Cake

1 box butter cake mix
1 (17 ounce) can fruit cocktail,
  undrained
1 (3 ounce) package instant
  lemon pudding
1 (3-1/2 ounce) can coconut,
  divided
4 eggs

1/4 cup oil
2/3 cup packed brown sugar
2/3 cup chopped pecans
Glaze:
1 stick margarine
3/4 cup sugar
1/4 cup milk

In a mixing bowl, combine cake mix, fruit cocktail, lemon pudding, one half the can of coconut, eggs and oil. Beat 4 minutes at medium speed. Pour into a deep 9 x 13 inch greased and floured pan. Combine brown sugar and pecans and sprinkle over top of cake. Bake at 325 degrees for 50 minutes or until cake tester comes out clean. Shortly before cake is done, melt margarine in a medium saucepan; add sugar and milk. Bring to a boil and cook for 2 minutes, stirring frequently. Add remaining coconut and pour over cake while cake is still hot.

Sifted flour means to sift flour before you measure.

Cream Cheese Pound Cake

2 sticks butter, softened (the
    real thing)
1 (8 ounce) package cream
    cheese, softened
1-3/4 cups sugar
1-1/2 teaspoons vanilla

5 eggs
2 cups flour
3/4 teaspoon baking powder
1/4 teaspoon salt
Powdered sugar

In your mixing bowl, beat together butter and cream cheese. Add sugar and
beat 4 to 5 minutes. Add vanilla and eggs, one at a time, beating 1 minute
after each addition. Add flour, baking powder and salt and beat at low speed
until well blended. Pour into a greased and floured 10 inch bundt pan. Bake
at 325 degrees for 60 to 65 minutes. Test with toothpick for doneness after 60
minutes. Cool 10 minutes and remove from pan and cool completely on wire
rack. Sprinkle top of cake with powdered sugar.

Banana Crunch Cake

1/2 stick margarine, melted
1 (15 ounce) can Pillsbury
    Coconut Pecan Frosting
1/4 cup finely chopped pecans
1 cup quick-cooking oats
1 cup sour cream
4 eggs
2 bananas, mashed
1 package yellow cake mix

3/4 cup water
1/3 cup oil
Icing:
3/4 cup powdered sugar
1 teaspoon vanilla
2 tablespoons margarine,
    melted
1/4 cup finely chopped pecans

In a medium bowl, combine the first 4 ingredients and set aside. In a large
mixing bowl, combine remaining ingredients except icing, and beat 3 minutes
at medium speed. Grease and flour a large tube pan. Pour 1/3 of the batter
into the tube pan. By tablespoonfuls, place 1/2 of the coconut-pecan mixture
in the batter around the tube, not touching the sides of the pan. Pour another
1/3 of the batter in pan and repeat the last half of the coconut-pecan mixture.
And finally pour the last 1/3 of the batter over top. Bake at 350 degrees for 1
hour and 5 minutes. For the icing: mix all ingredients together except the
pecans. Stir until smooth. Ice top of cake, letting some drip down the sides of
the cake. Sprinkle pecans over top.

*To prevent a cake from sticking to a plate,
sift powdered sugar on the plate before
placing fresh cake on it.*

Jan,

I love you,

Jake

Cinnamon Pound Cake

3 cups sugar
3 sticks margarine
1 (3 ounce) package cream
    cheese, softened
1 teaspoon vanilla
5 eggs
3 cups flour
1/4 teaspoon baking powder
1 teaspoon cinnamon

1 cup milk
1/3 cup brown sugar
1 tablespoon cinnamon
Glaze:
1-1/4 cups powdered sugar
1 teaspoon vanilla
2 tablespoons milk
1/4 teaspoon cinnamon

In your mixing bowl, cream together sugar, margarine, cream cheese and vanilla. Add eggs, one at a time, beating well after each addition. Mix flour, baking powder and cinnamon together. Add half of flour mixture to cream cheese mixture; beat well. Add milk; beat. Add remaining flour; beat well. In a small bowl, mix brown sugar and cinnamon. Pour 1/3 of the batter in a greased and floured tube pan. Sprinkle 1/2 sugar-cinnamon over batter. Pour in another 1/3 batter; sprinkle remaining sugar-cinnamon. Add remaining batter. Bake at 350 degrees for 1 hour and 10 minutes. Test with toothpick for doneness. Let cake cool. For glaze, mix powdered sugar, vanilla, milk and cinnamon. Pour glaze over cake, letting a little drizzle down sides of cake.

Amaretto Cake

1-1/2 cups sliced almonds
1 box yellow cake mix
1 (3-3/4 ounce) box vanilla
    pudding mix
3 eggs
1/3 cup oil
1/4 cup Amaretto

3/4 cup orange juice
1-1/2 teaspoons almond extract
Glaze:
4 tablespoons margarine
3/4 cup sugar
1/4 cup water
1/3 cup Amaretto

Spread almonds on a baking sheet and place in oven for 8 to 10 minutes at 325 degrees. Remove and set aside. Grease and flour a bundt pan; sprinkle 1/2 cup almonds on bottom of pan. In mixing bowl, combine cake mix, pudding mix, eggs, oil, Amaretto, orange juice and almond extract. Mix and beat until fluffy. Fold in remaining almonds; pour into bundt pan and cook 1 hour at 325 degrees (test cake with toothpick for doneness). Invert on cake plate. For glaze: mix margarine, sugar and water in a saucepan. Bring to a boil; boil 2 minutes. Add Amaretto. Prick cake with toothpick and spoon glaze over cake.

Lemon Apricot Pound Cake

1 (3.4 ounce) package instant
    lemon pudding mix
1 cup apricot nectar
1 box lemon cake mix
3/4 cup oil
1 tablespoon lemon extract
4 eggs

Icing:
2 cups powdered sugar
1 teaspoon lemon juice
2 tablespoons apricot nectar
2 tablespoons margarine,
    melted

In a small bowl mix pudding with the apricot nectar and let set while mixing the rest of ingredients. In mixing bowl, combine the cake mix, oil, lemon extract and 1 egg; beat well. Add the other eggs one at a time, beating after each addition. Add the pudding-apricot nectar mixture and beat. Pour batter into a greased and floured tube pan. Cook at 350 degrees for 40 minutes. Test with toothpick for doneness. Take out of pan immediately. Cool. For the icing: mix all ingredients together and blend well. Ice cake. If icing is a little too thick, add more apricot nectar.

Butterscotch Heaven

Crust:
1 stick margarine, melted
1-1/2 cups graham cracker
    crumbs
1/3 cup brown sugar
First and third layers:
1 (8 ounce) cream cheese,
    softened
1 can sweetened condensed
    milk
1/2 teaspoon almond extract
1 (12 ounce) container Cool
    Whip

Second layer:
1 stick margarine
2 (2 ounce) packages sliced
    almonds
1 cup coconut
1 (8 ounce) jar butterscotch
    topping
3/4 cup graham cracker crumbs
Topping:
1 (8 ounce) jar butterscotch
    topping

In a mixing bowl, mix together all crust ingredients together. Pat into a greased 9 x 13 inch baking pan. Bake at 350 degrees for 12 to 14 minutes or until it is lightly browned. For first layer: in mixing bowl, cream together cream cheese, condensed milk and almond extract until smooth. Fold in Cool Whip. Pour 1/2 of this mixture onto cooled crust. Chill in freezer for about 30 minutes. For second layer: melt margarine in a saucepan; add almonds, coconut, butterscotch topping and graham crackers. Mix. Sprinkle over cream cheese layer. For third layer: pour remaining cream cheese mixture over almond-butterscotch layer. Freeze. When frozen, pour remaining jar of butterscotch over top and swirl. Return to freezer. Take out of freezer 5 or 10 minutes before serving.

Strawberry Pineapple Fiesta

1-1/4 cups flour
1/3 cup packed brown sugar
1 stick margarine, softened
1/2 cup chopped pecans
First layer:
3/4 cup sugar
3 tablespoons cornstarch
1 (15-1/2 ounce) can crushed
    pineapple, undrained
Second layer:
1 (8 ounce) package cream
    cheese, softened

1-1/2 cups powdered sugar
1 (8 ounce) carton Cool Whip
Third layer:
1/2 cup sugar
3 tablespoons cornstarch
2 (10 ounce) packages frozen
    sweetened strawberries
Topping:
1 cup heavy cream
1/3 cup powdered sugar

In a mixing bowl, combine and mix flour, sugar and margarine. Beat until crumbly. Add pecans. Pat into a greased 9 x 13 inch baking pan. Bake at 350 degrees for about 13 to 14 minutes. Cool. First layer: in a saucepan, combine sugar and cornstarch. Add pineapple: cook on medium heat until thickened. Pour over crumb crust. Place in freezer until next layer is ready. For second layer: in mixing bowl, beat together the cream cheese and powdered sugar; fold in Cool Whip. Pour over the pineapple layer. Place in freezer for about 30 minutes. For third layer: in a saucepan, combine sugar and cornstarch; mix. Add strawberries and cook on medium heat until thickened. Pour over cream cheese layer. Freeze. Whip heavy cream until thickened; add sugar and mix. Cover the top with whipped cream. Remove from freezer 15 minutes before serving.

Ice Cream Cake

36 to 40 Lady Fingers
First layer:
3 cups vanilla ice cream, softened
1 (6 ounce) can frozen orange
    juice, undiluted
Second layer:
4 tablespoons cornstarch
1-1/2 cups sugar
1 (8 ounce) can crushed
    pineapple, undrained

1 (12 ounce) package frozen
    raspberries, thawed
Third layer:
3 cups vanilla ice cream,
    softened
1 teaspoon almond extract
1 teaspoon rum extract
10 maraschino cherries, chopped
1/2 cup chopped pecans

Line Lady Fingers around a 9 inch springform pan. Place Lady Fingers on bottom of pan. In a mixing bowl, mix softened ice cream and orange juice concentrate. Mix and pour over Lady Fingers. Place in freezer until next layer is ready. For second layer: in a saucepan, mix cornstarch and sugar. Add pineapple; stir. On medium heat, cook, stirring constantly, until thickened. Add raspberries and mix. Cool and pour over first layer. Freeze 5 or 6 hours before putting on third layer. For third layer: mix all ingredients together and pour over second layer. Freeze several hours before slicing. Serves 16.

Peanut Magic

1 cup flour
1 stick margarine
1/4 cup sugar
2/3 cup dry roasted peanuts,
   chopped, divided
1 (8 ounce) package cream
   cheese, softened
1 cup powdered sugar
1/3 cup crunchy peanut butter

1 (12 ounce) container Cool
   Whip, divided
1 (3 ounce) package instant
   vanilla pudding
3 cups milk, divided
1 teaspoon vanilla
1 (3 ounce) package instant
   chocolate pudding

In your mixing bowl, combine flour, margarine and sugar and beat until mixture becomes crumbly. Add 1/3 cup chopped peanuts. Pat into a greased and floured 9 x 13 inch baking pan. Bake at 350 degrees for 13 to 14 minutes. Let cool. Using the mixing bowl again, beat the cream cheese until creamy; add powdered sugar; mix. Add the peanut butter; mix. Fold in 1 cup of the Cool Whip. Pour this mixture into the baked crust and smooth out. Prepare the vanilla pudding with 1-1/2 cups milk and vanilla; pour onto the cream cheese mixture. Prepare the chocolate pudding with remaining milk and pour onto the vanilla mixture. Last, top with the remaining Cool Whip. Sprinkle on remaining 1/3 cup chopped peanuts. Refrigerate.

Ice Box Dessert

1 pound vanilla wafers,
   crushed to make crumbs
1/2 stick margarine, melted
1-3/4 cups milk
1 pound marshmallows

1 cup whipping cream,
   whipped
1 (15-1/2 ounce) can crushed
   pineapple, drained

Mix together the vanilla wafers and margarine. Pour 3/4 of the vanilla wafers into a greased 9 x 13 inch dish. Pat down to make crust. In a medium saucepan, scald milk (do not bring to boiling point) and add marshmallows; keep on low heat while stirring until marshmallows are melted. Cool to room temperature. Fold in whipped cream and pineapple. Pour over crust. Sprinkle with remaining vanilla wafer crumbs. Refrigerate. To serve, cut in squares. Serves 12.

To make 1 cup buttermilk, add 1 tablespoon white vinegar or lemon juice and let stand 5 minutes.

White Chocolate Cheesecake

Crumb Crust:
1-1/2 cups graham cracker
    crumbs
3 tablespoons sugar
6 tablespoons margarine,
    melted
1/4 cup chopped pecans
Filling:
6 ounces white chocolate
3/4 cup whipping cream,
    divided

2 (8 ounce) packages cream
    cheese, softened
3/4 cup, plus 2 tablespoons
    sugar
1 teaspoon vanilla
4 eggs
Sour cream topping:
1-1/2 cups sour cream
1/4 cup sugar
1 teaspoon vanilla
Grated white chocolate

Combine crumbs, sugar, margarine and pecans and place in a buttered springform pan. Using the back of a spoon, press mixture evenly in pan. Bake at 350 degrees for 10 minutes. Cool. Combine the white chocolate and 1/2 cup whipping cream in a double boiler until chocolate has melted. Stir until smooth. In a mixing bowl, beat cream cheese with remaining 1/4 cup whipping cream at low speed until smooth. Gradually beat in sugar and vanilla. Beat in eggs one at a time and beat until smooth. Gradually fold in white chocolate. Pour into cooled crust and bake at 325 degrees for 1 hour and 10 minutes. Cool for about 15 minutes. Turn oven temperature to 425 degrees. Combine sour cream, sugar and vanilla and pour over cheesecake. Bake 7 minutes. Remove from oven. Cool. Sprinkle grated white chocolate over top of cake. Refrigerate.

Strawberry Cheesecake

1-1/2 cups graham cracker
    crumbs
1 stick margarine, melted
3 tablespoons sugar
3 (8 ounce) packages cream
    cheese, softened
1-1/2 cups sugar
5 eggs

1 tablespoon vanilla
Strawberry topping:
2 cups whole fresh
    strawberries
2-1/4 cups sugar
1 tablespoon cornstarch
1 tablespoon milk

Combine graham cracker crumbs, margarine and sugar. Press into the bottom of a 9 inch springform pan. In a mixing bowl combine the cream cheese and sugar and beat for about 10 minutes. Add the eggs and vanilla and beat until well blended. Pour into the springform pan and bake at 350 degrees for 1 hour or until set. For topping: in a bowl, marinate the strawberries in the sugar. Let stand about 3 hours in refrigerator. Drain marinade into a saucepan; add the cornstarch and milk and heat. Simmer until mixture thickens. Cool and add the strawberries. Chill. Serve topping over each slice of cheesecake.

Pies

Outa Sight Pie

1 (14 ounce) can sweetened
    condensed milk
1 (21 ounce) can lemon pie
    filling

1 (20 ounce) can crushed
    pineapple, well drained
1 (8 ounce) carton Cool Whip
2 cookie flavored pie crusts*

In a large mixing bowl, combine the condensed milk and lemon pie filling and mix well. Add the well drained pineapple and Cool Whip and gently fold into pie filling mixture. Pour into 2 pie crusts. Refrigerate several hours before slicing. Eat one pie and freeze the other. *You can also use the graham cracker crust.

Margarita Pie

1 (14 ounce) can sweetened
    condensed milk
2 egg yolks
1/2 cup sugar
1/3 cup fresh lime juice
1-1/2 ounces Tequila
1 ounce Cointreau or Triple
    Sec

2 egg whites
1 (9 inch) graham cracker crust
1/4 cup sugar
1/2 cup whipping cream,
    whipped
Lime slices

In a medium size mixing bowl, combine the sweetened condensed milk, egg yolks, sugar, lime juice, tequila and Cointreau (or Triple Sec) and mix well. Beat egg whites until slightly stiff and fold them into the egg-sugar mixture. Spoon mixture into the graham cracker crust. Bake at 350 degrees for 25 minutes or until set. Let pie cool. Fold sugar into the whipped cream and spread over cooled pie. Refrigerate pie several hours before serving. Garnish each piece of pie with a thin lime slice.

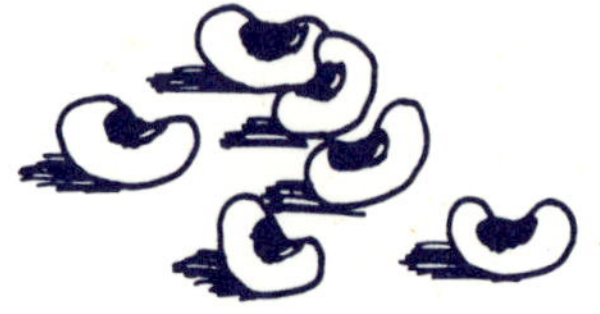

Sprinkle an equal mixture of sugar and flour into a pastry shell before filling to keep fruit from baking through the bottom of the shell.

Chocolate Pecan Pie

4 tablespoons margarine
3 ounces semisweet chocolate
1 cup light corn syrup
2/3 cup sugar
1-1/4 teaspoons vanilla

1/4 teaspoon salt
3 large eggs
1 cup pecan halves
1 unbaked 9 inch pie shell

In a medium saucepan, melt margarine with the chocolate, stirring until smooth. Remove from heat and beat in corn syrup, sugar, vanilla, salt and eggs. Mix well. Place pecans on bottom of pie shell. Pour chocolate mixture over the pecans. Bake at 350 degrees for 50 to 55 minutes or until knife inserted at the edge comes out clean.

Pecan Pie

2 tablespoons flour
2 tablespoons margarine,
    softened
3 eggs, beaten
2/3 cup sugar

1 cup corn syrup
1 tablespoon vanilla
Pinch of salt
1 cup pecans
1 (9 inch) pie shell, uncooked

In a mixing bowl, blend flour and margarine together. Add eggs, sugar, corn syrup, vanilla, salt and pecans. Pour into pie crust and bake at 350 degrees for 10 minutes. Reduce heat to 250 degrees and bake 1 hour and 15 minutes.

Egg whites beat better at room temperature.

Frozen Coffee Pie

1/3 cup white corn syrup
1/3 cup chunky peanut butter
2 cups Rice Krispies

2 pints coffee ice cream
Semi-sweet chocolate, shaved

In a medium mixing bowl, mix corn syrup and peanut butter together. Add Rice Krispies and mix well with wooden spoon. Press out in a 9 inch pie plate to make pie shell. Spread ice cream in shell. Sprinkle shaved chocolate over top. Keep in freezer. Remove from freezer 5 minutes before slicing.

Hershey Pie

6 plain Hershey bars
18 large marshmallows
1/2 cup milk
1 cup whipping cream,
   whipped

1/2 cup chopped pecans
1/2 cup coconut (optional)
1 (9 inch) baked pie crust

In a double boiler, melt Hershey bars and marshmallows in milk. Mix well. Cool and fold in whipped cream and pecans. Pour into pie crust. Refrigerate at least 8 hours before slicing.

A meringue topping should touch the edge of the crust; otherwise, it may shrink from the sides.

Pineapple Cheese Pie

1 (14 ounce) can condensed
   milk
1/4 cup lemon juice
1 (3 ounce) package cream
   cheese, softened

1 (8 ounce) can crushed
   pineapple, well drained
1 graham cracker pie crust
Cool Whip

In a mixing bowl, combine condensed milk, lemon juice and cream cheese and beat mixture until smooth. Fold in well drained pineapple and mix. Pour into the prepared graham cracker crust. Chill 8 hours before slicing. Serve with a dab of Cool Whip.

Tumbleweed Pie

1/2 gallon vanilla ice cream,
   softened
1/4 cup plus 1 tablespoon
   Kahlua
1/4 cup plus 1 tablespoon
   Amaretto

1 (10 inch) chocolate cookie
   crust
1 package slivered almonds
Chocolate shavings

Place ice cream, Kahlua and Amaretto in blender and blend. Pour into pie crust. Sprinkle almonds over top and freeze. When ready to serve, set out of freezer about 10 minutes before slicing. Garnish with chocolate shavings.

To substitute 1 square unsweetened chocolate, use 3 tablespoons cocoa plus 1 tablespoon margarine.

Grasshopper Pie

24 creme-filled chocolate
  cookies, crushed
1/4 cup margarine, melted
1 (7 ounce) jar marshmallow
  creme

1/4 cup Creme de Menthe
  liqueur
1 cup whipping cream,
  whipped

Combine cookie crumbs and margarine. Reserve 1/2 cup crumbs for topping. Press rest of crumbs into a 9 inch pie plate. In a medium bowl, mix together the marshmallow creme with the Creme de Menthe; blend well. Fold in whipped cream. Pour into crust and freeze. Sprinkle remaining crumbs on top and freeze.

Apple Pie Special

1 can sliced apples for pies,
  drained
1 tablespoon lemon juice
1/2 teaspoon nutmeg
3/4 teaspoon cinnamon
3/4 cup sugar
1/4 cup seedless raisins
1 (9 inch) unbaked pie crust
1 cup packed brown sugar

1/4 stick margarine, melted
2 tablespoons cornstarch
1/2 cup chopped pecans
Milk
Hard sauce:
1 stick margarine
1-1/2 cups powdered sugar
1 tablespoon boiling water
2 teaspoons rum or brandy

In a bowl, combine apples, lemon juice, nutmeg, cinnamon, sugar and raisins. Pour into one of the pie crusts. In a bowl, combine brown sugar, margarine, flour and pecans. Sprinkle over apple mixture. Top with second pie crust. Attach edges of the two pastries and flute with fingers. Prick top of pastry with a fork. Brush pastry with milk. Bake at 400 degrees for 10 minutes; reduce temperature to 325 degrees and bake for 30 to 35 minutes or until lightly browned. For hard sauce, mix all ingredients together. Pour over slices of pie when ready to serve.

Strawberry Pie

1 (10 ounce) package frozen
  strawberries, thawed
24 large marshmallows

1 cup whipping cream,
  whipped
1 graham cracker pie crust

Drain strawberries, reserving juice. Combine juice and marshmallows in a saucepan; cook over low heat until melted. Cool. Fold in whipped cream and strawberries. Pour into pie shell. Chill overnight.

Gypsy Pie

1/2 cup packed dates, cut in
   small pieces
Flour
4 egg whites, room
   temperature
1 cup plus 1 tablespoon sugar
1 teaspoon baking powder
1/4 teaspoon salt
3/4 teaspoon cream of tartar

1 teaspoon vanilla
3/4 cup graham cracker crumbs
1 cup chopped pecans
Topping:
1 cup whipping cream
3 tablespoons powdered sugar
1 teaspoon vanilla
1/4 cup chopped pecans

Dredge dates in flour, separating all pieces well. Shake excess flour off dates. Set aside. In a large mixing bowl, beat egg whites until stiff and glossy (several minutes). Combine sugar, baking powder, salt and cream of tartar. Gradually add sugar mixture to egg whites; continue beating until sugar is dissolved. Test by rubbing a tiny bit of egg whites between your fingers — it should feel smooth. Add vanilla; mix. Gently fold in the graham cracker crumbs, dates and 1 cup pecans. Do not overmix — just have cracker crumbs barely moist. Spread into a slightly greased 9 inch pie plate. Do not cover rim of pie plate. Bake at 325 degrees for 35 minutes or until lightly golden on top. Cool and place in refrigerator for 2 hours. For topping: whip cream and gradually add sugar and vanilla and continue whipping until peaks hold firm. Mound topping on pie and garnish with the 1/4 cup chopped pecans.

Peachy Ginger Cobbler

2 tablespoons cornstarch
2 tablespoons margarine
1/3 cup water
1-1/2 cups sugar
1/4 teaspoon cinnamon
3 cups fresh peaches, peeled
   and sliced
1/4 cup chopped crystalized
   ginger (no substitutions)

Topping:
1 cup flour
1/2 cup sugar
1/2 cup packed brown sugar
1/4 teaspoon salt
1/2 teaspoon baking powder
1 egg
1/2 stick margarine, melted
1 cup chopped pecans

In a saucepan, combine cornstarch, margarine, water, sugar and cinnamon. Heat, stirring constantly until mixture has thickened. Stir in peaches and crystalized ginger. Pour into a greased 8 x 12 inch baking dish. For topping, mix all ingredients together. Dot teaspoonfuls over peaches. Bake at 350 degrees for 40 to 45 minutes or until golden brown. Serves 8.

Lemon Freeze

2 eggs, separated
1 can Eagle Brand sweetened
    condensed milk
1/3 cup lemon juice
3 tablespoons sugar

1 (8 inch) graham cracker pie
    crust
3 double graham crackers,
    crushed
1 tablespoon sugar

In a medium mixing bowl, beat egg yolks until lemon-colored. Add condensed milk and lemon juice and stir until thickened. Beat egg whites until stiff but not dry. Beat in the 3 tablespoons sugar and fold gently into the condensed milk mixture. Pour into the pie crust. Mix crushed graham crackers and 1 tablespoon sugar and sprinkle over pie. Freeze. When ready to serve, take pie out of freezer about 10 minutes before slicing and serving.

Fruit Fajitas

1 can prepared fruit pie filling
10 small or 8 large flour
    tortillas
2 cups water

1-1/2 cups sugar
1-1/2 sticks margarine
1 teaspoon almond flavoring

Divide fruit equally on tortillas, roll up and place in a 9 x 13 baking dish. Mix together water, sugar and margarine in saucepan and bring to a boil. Add almond flavoring and pour over flour tortillas. Place in refrigerator and let soak 1 to 24 hours. Bake 350 degrees for 20 to 25 minutes until brown and bubbly.

Use a potato peeler when you need to make chocolate curls.

Peanut Butter Pie

1 quart vanilla ice cream,
    slightly softened
1/2 cup chunky peanut butter

1/2 cup unsalted peanuts,
    crushed
1-1/2 tablespoons vanilla
1 graham cracker pie crust

In a large mixing bowl, combine the softened ice cream, peanut butter, peanuts and vanilla and stir. It doesn't have to be completely mixed. Pour into pie crust and freeze for several hours before serving. Take out of freezer 5 minutes before slicing.

Lemonade Pie

1 (6 ounce) can frozen
    lemonade, thawed
1 can Eagle Brand condensed
    milk

6 ounces Cool Whip
1 graham cracker pie crust

Mix together the lemonade and condensed milk. Then fold in the Cool Whip and spread in pie crust. Freeze. When ready to serve, set out of freezer for 5 to 10 minutes before slicing.

Frozen Yogurt Pie

1/2 cup boiling water
1 (7.2 ounce) package Betty
    Crocker fluffy white
    frosting mix

2 (8 ounce) cartons strawberry
    yogurt
1 graham cracker pie crust
Fresh strawberries

In a medium mixing bowl, pour boiling water over frosting mix; beat at high speed on electric mixer for 5 minutes or until stiff peaks form. Fold in yogurt and pour into crust. Freeze. Before serving, remove from freezer 5 or 10 minutes before slicing. Garnish with fresh strawberries.

Cherry Crunch

1 can cherry pie filling
1 package white cake mix
1/2 cup pecans, chopped

1 stick margarine, melted
vanilla ice cream

Spread pie filling over the bottom of a buttered 9 x 13 inch baking dish. In a mixing bowl, combine the cake mix, pecans and margarine and mix well. Sprinkle over the pie filling and bake at 350 degrees for 35 minutes or until golden brown. Serve with vanilla ice cream.

Bars and Squares

Grasshopper Brownies

4 squares unsweetened
   chocolate
2 sticks margarine
2 cups sugar
3 large eggs, lightly beaten
1 cup flour
1 teaspoon vanilla
1 teaspoon salt
1 cup chopped pecans

First Icing Layer:
3 cups powdered sugar
2 tablespoons margarine,
   melted
4 tablespoons green Creme de
   Menthe*
1 tablespoon milk
Second Icing Layer:
4 squares semi-sweet chocolate
4 tablespoons margarine

In a saucepan, melt chocolate and margarine. In mixing bowl, beat sugar and eggs. Pour in melted chocolate and margarine; mix. Add flour, vanilla, salt and pecans. Mix well and pour into a greased and floured 9 x 13 inch baking pan. Bake at 325 degrees for 30 minutes. Cool. For first icing layer, mix together powdered sugar, margarine, Creme de Menthe and milk. Ice cooled brownies. For second icing layer, melt chocolate and margarine in saucepan. Pour over Creme de Menthe layer and smooth out. Cut into bars. *If you don't want to use the Creme de Menthe, you will get about the same results if you use (for the first icing layer): 3 cups powdered sugar, 2 tablespoons melted margarine, 4 tablespoons milk, 1 teaspoon peppermint extract and some green food coloring.

Brownies

2/3 cup oil
2 cups sugar
1/3 cup corn syrup
3 eggs, slightly beaten
2 teaspoons vanilla
1/2 cup cocoa
1-1/2 cups flour
1/2 teaspoon salt
1 teaspoon baking powder

1 cup chopped pecans
Icing:
1-1/2 cups powdered sugar
1/3 cup cocoa
3 tablespoons margarine,
   melted
1 tablespoon milk
1 teaspoon vanilla

In a mixing bowl, beat together the oil, sugar, corn syrup, eggs and vanilla. Add cocoa, flour, salt and baking powder. Beat well. Fold in chopped pecans. Pour into a 9 x 9 inch greased and floured pan. Bake at 350 degrees for 40 to 45 minutes. Cool. For icing: mix all ingredients and beat until smooth. Spread over brownies. Makes 12 brownies.

Lemon Crumb Squares

1-1/4 sticks margarine
1/2 cup sugar
1/2 cup brown sugar
1-1/2 cups flour
1 teaspoon baking powder

1/2 teaspoon salt
1 cup quick-cooking oatmeal
1 can eagle Brand sweetened
   condensed milk
1/2 cup lemon juice

Cream margarine and sugars together in mixing bowl. Add dry ingredients and oatmeal and beat until the mix is crumbly. Spread half the mixture in an 8 x 12 inch greased baking dish and pat down. In a separate bowl mix sweetened condensed milk and the lemon juice and stir until the lemon juice is completely mixed. Pour over crumbs in baking dish; then cover with the remaining crumbs. Bake at 350 degrees for 25 minutes. Cool at room temperature and cut into squares Refrigerate.

Carmelitas

Crust:
1 cup flour
3/4 cup brown sugar
1/8 teaspoon salt
1 cup quick-cooking oats
1/2 teaspoon baking soda
1-1/2 sticks margarine, melted

Filling:
1 (6 ounce) package chocolate
   chips
3/4 cup chopped pecans
1 (12 ounce) jar caramel ice
   cream topping
3 tablespoons flour

Combine all crust ingredients together in a large mixing bowl, blending well with mixer to form crumbs. Press 2/3 of crumbs into a greased 9 x 13 inch baking pan. Bake at 350 degrees for 10 minutes. Remove from oven and sprinkle with chocolate chips and pecans. Blend caramel topping with flour and spread over ships and pecans. Sprinkle with remaining crumb mixture. Bake 20 minutes or until golden brown. Chill for 2 hours before cutting into squares.

Scotch Crunchies

1/2 cup crunchy peanut butter
1 (6 ounce) package
   butterscotch bits

3 cups pre-sweetened
   cornflakes
1/2 cup peanuts

Melt peanut butter and butterscotch bits in a large saucepan. Stir until butterscotch bits are melted. Stir in cereal and peanuts. Press into a greased 9 x 13 pan. Refrigerate until firm. Cut into squares.

Butter Pecan Turtle Bars

2 cups flour
3/4 cup packed light brown
   sugar
1 stick margarine, softened
1-1/2 cups pecans, lightly
   chopped

3/4 cup packed light brown
   sugar
1-1/3 sticks margarine
4 squares semi-sweet chocolate
1/2 stick margarine

In a large mixing bowl, combine flour, 3/4 cup brown sugar and margarine and blend until crumbly. Pat firmly into a greased 9 x 13 baking pan. Sprinkle pecans over unbaked crust. Set aside. In a small saucepan, combine 3/4 cup brown sugar and 1-1/3 sticks margarine. Cook over medium heat, stirring constantly. When mixture comes to a boil, boil for 1 minute, stirring constantly. Drizzle this caramel sauce over pecans and crust. Bake at 350 degrees for 18 to 20 minutes or until caramel layer is bubbly. Remove from oven and cool. In a saucepan, melt chocolate squares and margarine and stir until smooth. Pour over bars and spread around. Cool and cut into bars.

Pecan Cups

Shell:
2 sticks margarine
1 (8 ounce) package cream
   cheese, softened
Dash of salt
2 cups flour
Filling:

2 eggs, lightly beaten
1/4 cup sugar
1-1/4 cups packed brown sugar
3 tablespoons margarine,
   melted
1-1/4 cups chopped pecans
1/2 teaspoon vanilla

In a mixing bowl, beat margarine and cream cheese together until fluffy. Add salt and flour; mix well. Refrigerate dough until firm enough to handle. After chilling, form dough into little balls and press into bottoms and sides of 24 lightly buttered miniature muffin tins. For the filling, mix all ingredients and pour into the shells. Bake at 350 degrees for 30 minutes.

For an easy way to send iced cupcakes to school in the lunch box, split the cupcakes and put icing in the middle.

Butterscotch Brownies

3 cups packed brown sugar
2 sticks margarine, softened
3 eggs
3 cups flour
2 tablespoons baking powder
1/2 teaspoon salt
1-1/2 cups chopped pecans
1 cup coconut

Glaze:
1/2 cup brown sugar, packed
1/3 cup evaporated milk
1 stick margarine
1/8 teaspoon salt
1 cup powdered sugar
1/2 teaspoon vanilla

Combine and beat sugar and margarine until fluffy; add eggs and blend. Sift flour, baking powder and salt together and add to the other mixture 1 cup at a time. Add pecans and coconut. Spread batter into a large 11 x 17 well greased pan and bake at 350 degrees for 20 to 25 minutes. (Batter will be hard to spread.) For glaze: In a saucepan, combine the brown sugar, milk, margarine and salt and bring to a boil. Cool slightly and add powdered sugar and vanilla and beat until smooth. Spread over cooled brownies. Cut into squares.

Chewy Butterscotch Bars

1 cup packed brown sugar
1 stick margarine
2 eggs
1 teaspoon vanilla
1/2 cup flour

1 (3-3/4 ounce) package instant
   butterscotch pudding mix
1/4 teaspoon salt
3/4 cup quick-cooking oats
Powdered sugar

In a mixing bowl, beat together sugar and margarine. Add eggs and vanilla; beat well. Stir together flour, dry pudding mix and salt. Add to creamed mixture and mix well. Stir in oats; mix. Spread batter in a greased and floured 9 x 9 inch baking pan. Cool in pan. Sprinkle powdered sugar over top with shaker or sift through a tea strained. Cut into bars.

*If your children don't like nuts;
substitute Rice Krispies.*

Raspberry Almond Squares

1-1/2 cups flour
1/2 cup sugar
1/2 teaspoon baking powder
1/2 teaspoon cinnamon
1 stick margarine, softened
1 egg
1/2 teaspoon almond extract

1/2 cup ground almonds
3/4 cup raspberry jam
Icing:
1/2 cup powdered sugar
2 teaspoons milk
1/4 teaspoon almond extract

In a mixing bowl, combine flour, sugar, baking powder and cinnamon; cut in margarine. Mix in egg, almond extract and almonds. Divide dough in half. Press half in a greased and floured 9 x 9 inch baking pan. Spread on jam and top with other half dough; press down gently. Bake at 350 degrees for 35 to 40 minutes. Cool. For the icing, combine powdered sugar, milk and almond extract; stir until smooth. Drizzle over cooked squares. Cut into squares.

Pecan Bars

Crust:
3 cups flour
1-1/2 sticks margarine,
    softened
1/3 cup sugar
3/4 teaspoon salt
Filling:

4 eggs, beaten
1-1/2 cups brown sugar
1-1/2 cups light corn syrup
3 tablespoons margarine,
    melted
1-1/2 teaspoons vanilla
2-1/2 cups chopped pecans

With mixer, blend flour, margarine, sugar and salt; then press firmly in a greased 12 x 18 jelly-roll pan. Bake at 350 degrees about 25 minutes or until golden brown. For filling, mix all ingredients except pecans. Spread pecans over crust and pour egg mixture over baked layer and spread evenly. Bake at 350 degrees about 25 minutes more or until filling is set. Cool and cut into squares.

For quick homemade chocolate ice cream, use one 12 ounce carton Cool Whip, 2 cans Eagle Brand sweetened condensed milk and 2 quarts of chocolate milk. Pour into ice cream freezer and freeze.

Fudge Krispy Bars

1 (12 ounce) package milk
   chocolate chips
3/4 stick margarine
1/2 cup light corn syrup
1 teaspoon vanilla

1/4 cup peanut butter
1 cup powdered sugar
4-1/2 cups oven-t Rice Krispies
1/2 cup chopped pecans

Butter a 9 x 13 inch pan. In a large saucepan, combine chips, margarine and corn syrup. Stir over low heat until melted. Remove from heat and add vanilla, peanut butter and powdered sugar. Mix. Stir in cereal and pecans and mix well. Spread in buttered pan. Chill until firm. Cut into bars and store in refrigerator.

Raspberry Shortbread Bars

1 box butter cake mix
2/3 cup finely chopped pecans
1/2 stick margarine, softened
1 egg

1 (10 ounce) jar raspberry
   preserves
3/4 cup powdered sugar
1 tablespoon water
1/2 teaspoon almond extract

In a large mixing bowl, combine cake mix, pecans, margarine and egg. Mix at low speed until crumbly. Press mixture into bottom of a greased and floured 9 x 13 inch baking pan. Spread with preserves. Bake at 350 degrees for 25 minutes or until edges are light brown. Cool. Combine powdered sugar, water and almond extract; mix until smooth. Drizzle over warm shortbread. Cut into bars.

Apricot Squares

1-1/2 cups flour
1 teaspoon baking powder
1/4 teaspoon salt
1-1/2 cups quick cooking oats

1-1/4 cups packed brown sugar
1-1/2 sticks margarine
1-1/4 cups apricot

In a large mixing bowl, mix together flour, baking powder, salt, oats and brown sugar. Cut in margarine until very crumbly. Pat 2/3 crumb mixture into a greased 9 x 13 inch baking pan. Spread with jam and sprinkle remaining crumbs on top. Bake at 350 degrees for 35 minutes. Cool before cutting.

Cookies

Sugar Cookies

1 cup sugar
1 cup powdered sugar
2 sticks margarine, softened
1 cup oil
2 eggs
1 tablespoon vanilla
1 teaspoon cream of tartar
1 teaspoon baking soda
4-1/2 cups flour
Sugar

In mixing bowl, beat together sugars, margarine, oil, eggs and vanilla. Add all dry ingredients and mix well. Refrigerate several hours or overnight. When ready to bake, make small balls and place on a cookie sheet. Press down with the bottom of a glass that is dipped in water. Sprinkle sugar on top of cookies. Bake at 350 degrees for 8 to 10 minutes. Do not brown.

Chocolate Pearls

2-1/4 cups flour
2/3 cup cocoa
1 teaspoon baking soda
1/2 teaspoon salt
2 sticks margarine, softened
3/4 cup sugar
2/3 cup firmly packed brown
   sugar
1 teaspoon vanilla
2 eggs
1 (10 ounce) package Nestle's
   Premier White Toll House
   Treasures baking pieces
   (white chocolate)

In a small bowl, combine flour, cocoa, baking soda and salt and set aside. In a large mixing bowl, beat margarine, sugar, brown sugar and vanilla until creamy. Add eggs, one at a time, beating well after each addition. Gradually add dry ingredients and mix well. Stir in (white chocolate) baking pieces and mix. Drop by rounded tablespoonfuls onto an ungreased cookie sheet. Bake at 350 degrees for 9 to 10 minutes. Makes about 30 large cookies.

Haystacks

1 (12 ounce) package
   butterscotch morsels
2 cups chow mein noodles
1 cup dry roasted peanuts

In a medium saucepan, heat butterscotch morsels over low heat until completely melted. Add noodles and peanuts and stir until each piece is coated. Drop from spoon onto wax paper. Cool.

Date and Rice Krispy Cookies

1 cup sugar
1/2 stick margarine
2 eggs
1 package dates, cut up

3 cups Rice Krispies
1 cup very finely chopped
    pecans*

In a large saucepan, combine sugar, margarine, eggs and dates. Bring to a boil, reduce heat and cook 5 minutes, stirring constantly. Then add Rice Krispies and mix well. Rub shortening on hands and with a heaping tablespoon of cookie dough, form into balls and roll in chopped pecans. *Coconut could be used instead of pecans.

Butterscotch Cookies

2 sticks margarine, softened
3/4 cup brown sugar
3/4 cup sugar
2 eggs
2 teaspoons vanilla
3 cups flour

1 teaspoon baking soda
1/2 teaspoon salt
1/4 teaspoon cinnamon
1 (12 ounce) package
    butterscotch morsels

In a large mixing bowl, cream margarine and sugars together. Add eggs and vanilla. Mix in the flour, baking soda, salt and cinnamon and mix well. Stir in butterscotch morsels and drop by teaspoonfuls onto an ungreased cookie sheet. Bake at 350 degrees for 10 to 15 minutes or until light brown.

*To maintain egg quality, store the egg
with the larger end up.*

Surprise Cookies

1-1/3 cups graham cracker
   crumbs
2 cups quick oats
2 cups sugar
2 tablespoons cocoa

1/2 cup milk
1/2 cup margarine
1/2 cup peanut butter
1 teaspoon vanilla

Combine graham cracker crumbs and oats. Set aside. In a large saucepan, mix sugar, cocoa, milk and margarine. Bring to a boil and cook for 1 minute. Remove from heat and stir in peanut butter and vanilla. Add crumbs-oats mixture quickly; blend. Drop by teaspoonfuls onto waxed paper. Cool.

The Ultimate Chocolate Chip Cookie

3/4 cup shortening
1-1/4 cups firmly packed
   brown sugar
2 tablespoons milk
2 teaspoons vanilla
1 egg

1-3/4 cups flour
1 teaspoon salt
3/4 teaspoon baking soda
1 cup semi-sweet chocolate
   chips
1 cup chopped pecans

Cream shortening, sugar, milk and vanilla in a large bowl. Blend until creamy. Add egg and mix. Add flour, salt and baking soda to the creamed mixture and stir well. Stir in chocolate chips and pecans. Drop rounded tablespoonfuls of dough onto an ungreased baking sheet. Bake at 375 degrees for 10 minutes for chewy cookies and 11 to 13 minutes for crisp cookies.

Marshmallow Treats

1/2 stick margarine
4 cups miniature
   marshmallows

1/2 cup chunky peanut butter
6 cups Rice Krispies cereal

In a large saucepan, melt margarine; add marshmallows and stir until melted. Remove from heat and add peanut butter. Mix well. Add Rice Krispies and stir until well coated. Using a buttered spatula, press mixture evenly into a buttered 9 x 13 inch pan. Cool. Cut in squares.

Party Kisses

3 egg whites
1 cup sugar
2 teaspoons vanilla

1/2 teaspoon almond extract
3-1/3 cups Frosted Flakes
1 cup chopped pecans

In a mixing bowl, beat egg whites until stiff. Gradually add sugar and extracts. Fold in Frosted Flakes and pecans. Drop by teaspoonfuls on a cookie sheet lined with waxed paper. Bake at 250 degrees for 40 minutes. Makes about 4 dozen.

Cream Cheese Cookies

1-1/2 sticks margarine,
   softened
1 (3 ounce) package cream
   cheese, softened
2 cups powdered sugar
1 teaspoon vanilla

1 tablespoon lemon juice
2 teaspoons grated lemon peel
2 cups flour
1 cup chopped pecans
Powdered sugar

Cream together margarine and cream cheese; beat until light and fluffy. Add sugar, vanilla, lemon juice and lemon peel; beat. Add flour, mixing well. Stir in pecans. Drop cookie dough by teaspoonfuls onto a greased cookie sheet. Bake at 300 degrees for 20 to 25 minutes. They do not need to brown. While hot, dip tops of cookies in powdered sugar.

Orange Fingers

3-1/4 cups vanilla wafer
   crumbs
1 (16 ounce) box powdered
   sugar
2 cups chopped pecans

1 (6 ounce) can frozen orange
   juice concentrate, thawed
1 stick margarine, melted
1 cup flaked coconut

Mix vanilla wafer crumbs, powdered sugar and pecans together. Stir in orange juice and margarine. Shape into 2 inch fingers and roll in coconut. Refrigerate.

Peanut Krispies

1 stick margarine
2 cups chunky peanut butter
1 (16 ounce) box powdered
    sugar

3-1/2 cups Rice Krispies
3/4 cup peanuts, chopped

In a large saucepan, melt margarine. Add peanut butter and mix well. Add powdered sugar, Rice Krispies and peanuts. Mix. Drop by teaspoonfuls onto wax paper.

The Best Peanut Butter Cookies

1 stick margarine, softened
1/4 cup shortening
1-1/4 cups chunky peanut
    butter
1/2 cup sugar
1 cup brown sugar

1 egg
1-1/2 cups flour
1/2 teaspoon baking powder
3/4 teaspoon baking soda
1/4 teaspoon salt

In a large mixing bowl, cream together the margarine, shortening, peanut butter, sugars and egg. Beat until well mixed and fluffy. Blend in dry ingredients. Using a large size cookie scoop, place cookies on a cookie sheet. Dip a fork in water and flatten just a little with a crisscross pattern. You want the cookies to remain kind-of fat and larger than most cookies. Bake at 350 degrees for about 12 minutes.

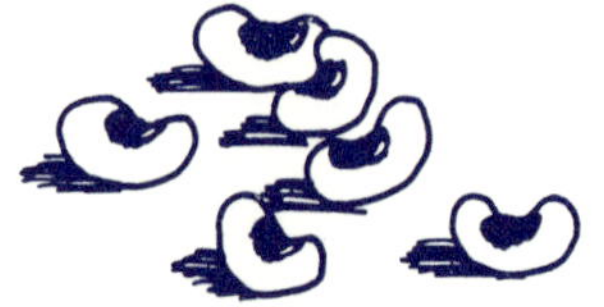

Use small juice cans, with both ends removed for cookie cutters. Before lifting the cutter from the cookie dough, sprinkle with sugar, nuts or candies into the top of the can to avoid spills.

Cinnamon Sticks

2 sticks margarine, softened
1 cup granulated sugar, plus 2
   tablespoons
1 egg yolk
2 cups flour

1 teaspoon vanilla
3 teaspoons cinnamon
Pinch of salt
1 egg white
3/4 cup chopped pecans

In your mixing bowl, combine all ingredients except the egg white and pecans. With your mixer, beat until a dough forms. Pat into a buttered 10 x 14 inch baking pan. Beat egg whites (no need to wash beaters) until frothy. Brush on cookie dough and top with pecans. Bake at 350 degrees for 25 minutes. Cut into long narrow strips as soon as they are removed from the oven. Remove from pan when cool.

Orange Drops

2 cups sugar
2 sticks margarine, softened
2 eggs
1/2 cup orange juice
1 cup sour cream
1 teaspoon vanilla
4-1/2 cups flour
1 teaspoon baking powder
1/2 teaspoon salt

Frosting:
1 cup confectioners sugar
3 tablespoons margarine,
   softened
2 tablespoons orange juice
1/2 teaspoon orange extract
1 drop yellow food coloring,
   optional

In a large mixing bowl, combine sugar, margarine, eggs, orange juice, sour cream and vanilla and mix well. Add dry ingredients until well mixed. Drop dough by teaspoonfuls 1 inch apart onto a greased cookie sheet. Bake at 350 degrees for 13 to 15 minutes; cookies will not brown so be careful not to overbake. Cool. Mix all frosting ingredients together until very smooth. Frost cookies.

Bake cookies on the top shelf of oven so they won't brown too much on the bottom.

Ginger Gems

1 stick margarine, softened
3/4 cup sugar
1 egg
1 tablespoon lemon juice

1-2/3 cups flour
1/2 teaspoon baking soda
1/2 cup finely chopped
  crystallized ginger

In a mixing bowl, beat together the margarine, sugar, egg and lemon juice. Beat 3 to 4 minutes. With mixer at low speed, gradually add flour and soda. Beat another 3 to 4 minutes. Fold in crystallized ginger. With a teaspoon, drop cookies onto a well greased baking sheet. Bake at 350 degrees for 13 to 15 minutes or until golden, but not brown.

Sierra Nuggets

2 sticks margarine
1 cup brown sugar
1-1/2 cups white sugar
1 tablespoon milk
2 teaspoons vanilla
2 eggs
1 cup crushed flake cereal
3 cups oatmeal
1-1/2 cups flour

1-1/4 teaspoons baking soda
1 teaspoon salt
2 teaspoons cinnamon
1/4 teaspoon nutmeg
1/8 teaspoon clove
1/2 cup coconut
2 cups chocolate chips
1 cup walnuts or pecans

In a large mixing bowl, cream together the margarine and sugars and beat in milk, vanilla and eggs. Then stir in flake cereal and oatmeal. Sift together the flour, baking soda, salt and seasonings. Gradually add to cookie mixture. Stir in coconut, chocolate chips and nuts. Drop by teaspoon on cookie sheet and bake at 350 degrees for 10 to 15 minutes.

Peanut Krispies

1 stick margarine
2 cups peanut butter
1 (16 ounce) box powdered
  sugar

3-1/2 cups Rice Krispies
3/4 cup peanuts, chopped

In a large saucepan, melt margarine. Add peanut butter and mix well. Add powdered sugar, Rice Krispies and peanuts. Mix. Drop by teaspoonfuls onto wax paper.

Shortbread Crunchies

2 sticks margarine
1 cup oil
1 cup sugar
1 cup brown sugar
1 egg
1 teaspoon vanilla
1 cup quick-cooking oats

3-1/2 cups sifted flour
1 teaspoon baking soda
1 teaspoon salt
1 cup crushed cornflakes
1 can coconut
1 cup chopped pecans

Cream together the margarine, oil and sugars; then add egg and vanilla and mix well. Add oats and dry ingredients and mix. Add the cornflakes, coconut and pecans last and mix. Drop by teaspoon on an ungreased cookie sheet. Flatten with fork dipped in water. Bake at 325 degrees for 15 minutes or until only slightly browned.

Oatmeal Crisps

1/2 cup margarine
1/2 cup brown sugar
1/2 cup sugar
1 egg
1 cup flour
1 teaspoon soda

1/2 teaspoon salt
1 cup quick-cooking oatmeal
1 cup Rice Krispies
1 cup coconut
1 teaspoon vanilla

Mix together margarine, sugars and egg. Beat well. Stir in remaining ingredients and mix well. Roll into 1 inch balls and place on greased cookie sheet. Bake at 350 degrees for 10 to 15 minutes or until golden brown.

Crunchy Oatmeal Cookies

1 cup sugar
1 cup packed brown sugar
1 cup shortening
2 eggs
1-3/4 cups flour
1 teaspoon baking powder

1 teaspoon baking soda
1/2 teaspoon cinnamon
1/4 teaspoon nutmeg
1-1/2 cups oatmeal
1 cup chopped pecans
2 teaspoons vanilla

Cream sugars, shortening and eggs; beat. Add remaining ingredients and mix. Roll into 1 inch balls and place on ungreased cookie sheet. Bake 10 to 12 minutes at 350 degrees.

Pralines

Praline Cake

1 cup quick-cooking oats
1 cup cold water
1 cup sugar
1-1/4 cups brown sugar
1 cup oil
2 eggs
1-1/2 cups flour
1 teaspoon baking soda

1 teaspoon cinnamon
1/4 teaspoon salt
Icing:
1 stick margarine
2 tablespoons milk
1 cup packed brown sugar
1 cup chopped pecans

In a small bowl combine the oats and water; set aside. In a larger mixing bowl, cream together the sugars, oil and eggs. Beat. Add oat mixture, flour, soda, cinnamon and salt. Mix well. Pour into a greased and floured 9 x 13 inch baking pan. Bake at 350 degrees for 35 minutes. For the icing: just before cake is done, combine margarine, milk and brown sugar in a saucepan. Bring to a boil and boil 1 minute. Add pecans; mix. Spread over hot cake.

Praline Ice Cream Cake

1 stick margarine
1 pint vanilla ice cream,
    softened
2 eggs
1-1/2 cups flour
2/3 cup sugar
1 tablespoon baking powder

1/2 teaspoon salt
1 cup graham cracker crumbs
1/2 cup sour cream
1 cup caramel ice cream
    topping
1/2 cup chopped pecans

Melt margarine in a large saucepan and add the ice cream, eggs, flour, sugar, baking powder, salt and graham cracker crumbs. Mix until smooth and pour into a greased and floured 9 x 13 inch baking pan. Bake at 350 degrees for 30 to 35 minutes. While cake is still warm, combine sour cream and ice cream topping and pour over cake. Top with the chopped pecans.

If pralines begin to get too hard before you can get candy dropped, add 1 teaspoon of water and stir; add more water if needed.

Praline Yams

1 (16 ounce) can sweet potatoes
2 tablespoons margarine,
    melted
3 tablespoons orange juice

1/2 cup packed brown sugar
1/4 cup chopped pecans
1/2 teaspoon cinnamon

Lightly grease a 1 quart glass baking dish. In a mixing bowl, mash the sweet potatoes. Add margarine and orange juice and blend thoroughly. Spoon into baking dish. Combine brown sugar, pecans and cinnamon and sprinkle over the sweet potato mixture. Bake at 350 degrees for 25 minutes Serves 4.

Praline and Orange Sauce

1/2 cup sugar
2/3 cup packed brown sugar
2 tablespoons flour
Dash salt
2/3 cup water
1 teaspoon grated orange peel

1/3 cup orange juice
1/2 cup miniature
    marshmallows
2 tablespoons margarine
1/2 cup chopped pecans
1 teaspoon vanilla

In a medium saucepan, stir together sugars, flour and salt. Stir in the water, orange peel and orange juice. Cook, stirring constantly, over medium heat until thickened and bubbly. Add marshmallows and margarine; cook and stir until melted. Remove from heat; add pecans and vanilla. Serve warm over ice cream or pound cake.

Praline Sauce

1-1/4 cups packed light brown
    sugar
1/4 cup light corn syrup
1/2 cup half and half or Milnot

2 tablespoons margarine
1 teaspoon vanilla
1/8 teaspoon salt
1 cup chopped pecans

Combine all ingredients in a saucepan. Cook over medium heat, stirring constantly, for 10 minutes or until sauce has thickened. Cool. Serve over ice cream, cheesecake or pound cake.

Praline Cheesecake

1-1/4 cups graham cracker
    crumbs
4 tablespoons sugar
4 tablespoons margarine,
    melted
3 (8 ounce) packages cream
    cheese, softened

1-1/4 cups packed dark brown
    sugar
2 tablespoons flour
3 large eggs
2 teaspoons vanilla
1/2 cup finely chopped pecans
Pecan halves
Maple syrup*

Combine crumbs, sugar and margarine; press into the bottom of a 9 inch springform pan. Bake at 350 degrees for 10 minutes. In mixing bowl, combine cream cheese, brown sugar and flour, mixing at medium speed on electric mixer until well blended. Add eggs, one at a time, mixing well after each addition. Blend in vanilla and stir in chopped pecans. Pour over crust. Bake at 350 degrees for 50 to 55 minutes. Loosen cake from rim of pan, but cool before removing rim of pan. Chill. Place pecan halves around the edge of the cake (about 1 inch from the edge) about an inch apart. Then pour syrup over top of cheesecake. When you slice the cheesecake, you might want to pour another teaspoon of the syrup over each slice so some will run down sides of the slice. *You could use the Praline Sauce (page 143) instead of the maple syrup.

Praline Ice Cream Pie

2 tablespoons margarine
1/3 cup packed brown sugar
1/3 cup chopped pecans
1 (9 inch) unbaked pie crust
1-1/4 cups vanilla ice cream,
    softened
1-1/2 cups cold milk

1 (3-3/4 ounce) package instant
    butterscotch pudding*
1 teaspoon vanilla
1 cup whipping cream
3 tablespoons powdered sugar
Chopped pecans

In a saucepan, melt the margarine, add brown sugar and pecans; mix. Sprinkle this mixture into the pie shell and bake at 400 degrees about 5 to 6 minutes or until lightly brown. Cool. In mixing bowl, combine the ice cream, milk, butterscotch pudding and vanilla. Beat at low speed until well blended, about 1 minute. Pour into the pie crust; chill several hours. Whip cream and add the powdered sugar. Top the pie with the whipped cream and spread around. Sprinkle a few pecans over whipped cream. Keep refrigerated. *Use instant butter pecan pudding if you can find it.

Praline Pumpkin Pie

1/3 cup packed brown sugar
2 tablespoons margarine,
 softened
1/3 cup chopped pecans
1 (9 inch) deep dish pie shell,
 unbaked
2 eggs
1 (16 ounce) can pumpkin
1-1/4 cups brown sugar

1 tablespoon flour
1/4 teaspoon ground cloves
3/4 teaspoon cinnamon
1/2 teaspoon ginger
1/2 teaspoon salt
1 cup half and half or Milnot
1 cup whipping cream
3 tablespoons powdered sugar

In a small bowl, blend together the brown sugar, margarine and pecans. Press into the pie shell. In mixing bowl, beat eggs until frothy and add remaining ingredients except whipping cream and powdered sugar. Pour mixture over the praline layer and bake at 350 degrees for 55 to 60 minutes or until tip of sharp knife comes out clean. Whip the cream and add powdered sugar. Serve pie with a dollop of whipped cream on each slice.

Praline Bars

1 box graham crackers
2 sticks butter

1-1/2 cups light brown sugar
1 cup chopped pecans

Line the bottom of a lightly greased cookie pan (one with sides) with a layer of uncrushed graham crackers. Melt butter in small saucepan and add brown sugar. Boil for 2 minutes. Remove from heat and add pecans. Pour and spread evenly over crackers. Bake 10 minutes at 350 degrees. Cut while warm.

Butter the inside top rim of a pan to keep candy from boiling over.

Pralines I

1 cup buttermilk
2 cups sugar
1 cup packed dark brown sugar
1 teaspoon baking soda
1/8 teaspoon salt

2/3 cup light corn syrup
2 teaspoons vanilla
2 tablespoons margarine,
    melted
2 cups pecan halves

In a large saucepan, cook buttermilk, sugar, brown sugar, baking soda, salt and corn syrup over medium to low heat, stirring occasionally. Insert candy thermometer into mixture and cook to 238 degrees (about 20 minutes). Remove from heat and mix in vanilla, margarine and pecans and beat until creamy and thick. Drop by tablespoonfuls onto buttered wax paper. Cool.

Pralines II

2 cups sugar
1/2 cup dark brown sugar
Dash of salt
2 tablespoons white corn syrup
2/3 cup evaporated milk

1/3 teaspoon soda
1 stick margarine
3 cups pecans, slightly broken
2 teaspoons vanilla

In a saucepan, combine the first 7 ingredients and bring to a hard boil, stirring until sugar dissolves. Cook to the soft ball stage (238 degrees on candy thermometer); it will probably take about 20 minutes of cooking. Stir real often. Remove from heat and add the pecans and vanilla and beat well. When candy begins to cool, drop from a tablespoonful onto buttered wax paper and cool.

Pralines III

2 cups light brown sugar
1 cup sugar
3/4 cup milk
Dash of salt

2-1/2 cups broken pecans
2 tablespoons margarine
1/2 teaspoon vanilla

Combine sugars, milk and salt in a large saucepan and bring to a boil. Boil for 10 minutes, stirring constantly. Add pecans; stir and boil for 10 minutes more. Remove from heat and add margarine and vanilla. Beat for 2 to 3 minutes. Drop by tablespoonfuls on a greased cookie sheet. Cool.

Pralines IV

1 cup sugar
1 cup light corn syrup
Pinch of salt
1/2 stick margarine

7/8 cup milk
2 cups pecans
1 teaspoon vanilla

Cook sugar, syrup and salt rapidly to boiling stage, stirring constantly. Gradually add margarine, milk and pecans, so that the mixture continues to boil. Cook over medium heat to firm boil stage, about 25 minutes, stirring constantly to keep mixture from sticking. Add vanilla and allow to stand until mixture stops bubbling. Beat a few minutes or until mixture begins to get stiff. Drop tablespoonfuls onto a well-buttered cookie sheet. Cool at room temperature.

Pralines V

2 cups sugar
1 cup brown sugar
1 stick margarine
1/4 cup light corn syrup

1 cup Milnot or evaporated
   milk
3 cups pecan halves

In a large saucepan, place all the ingredients except the pecans. Heat over medium heat, stirring constantly until the mixture boils. Continue boiling, at low heat until the soft ball stage (238 degrees) on a candy thermometer is reached (about 30 minutes). Stir often. Remove from heat and beat until creamy thick. Add pecans and drop by tablespoonfuls on wax paper. Cool. Store in air tight containers.

Quick Pralines

1 (3 ounce) box butterscotch
   Cook 'n Serve pudding
1 cup sugar
1/2 cup brown sugar

1/2 cup evaporated milk
2 cups pecan pieces
2 teaspoons vanilla

In a large saucepan, mix together butterscotch pudding, sugars and evaporated milk. Bring to a boil and boil, stirring constantly for 2 minutes. While still on burner, add the pecans and vanilla and boil 1-1/2 minutes stirring constantly. Beat until candy begins to cool and drop by tablespoonfuls on wax paper.

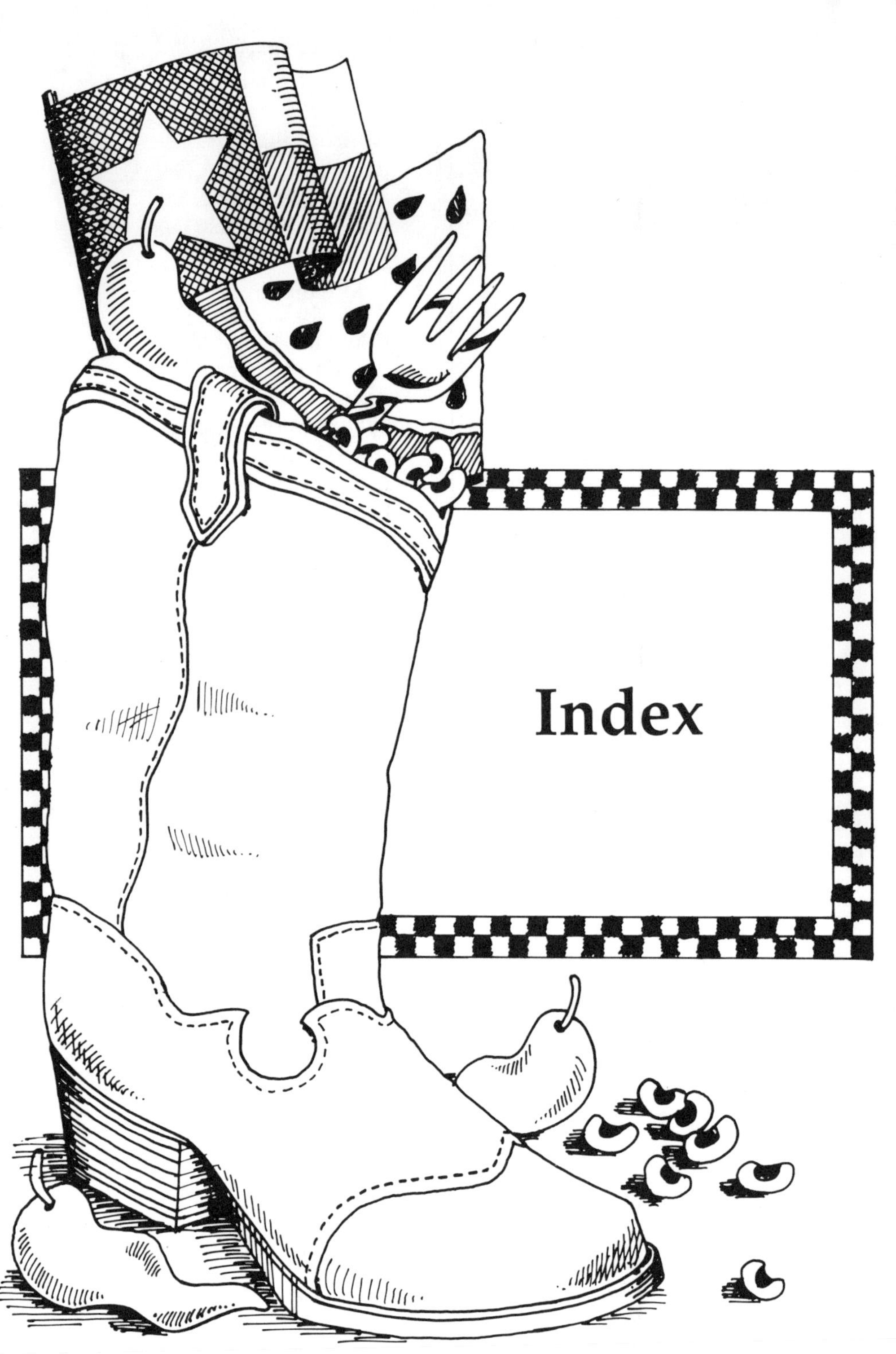
Index

ORDER FORM

Black-Eyed Peas To Pralines
Barbara C. Jones
1901 South Shore Drive
Bonham, Texas 75418
903/583-8898

Please send _____ copies of
Black-Eyed Peas to Pralines   @ $9.95 each, $________
      Postage and handling   @ $2.00 each, $________
      Texas residents add sales tax   @ $ .80 each, $________

Please send _____ copies of
Finders Keepers   @ $9.95 each, $________
      Postage and handling   @ $2.00 each, $________
      Texas residents add sales tax   @ $ .80 each, $________

Please send _____ copies of
A Little Taste of Texas   @ $6.95 each, $________
      Postage and handling   @ $1.75 each, $________
      Texas residents add sales tax   @ $ .52 each, $________

Please send _____ copies of
Southwest Sizzler   @ $6.95 each, $________
      Postage and handling   @ $1.75 each, $________
      Texas residents add sales tax   @ $ .52 each, $________

Total ________

Name ____

Address ____

City _________________ State _____________ Zip ______________

Telephone ____